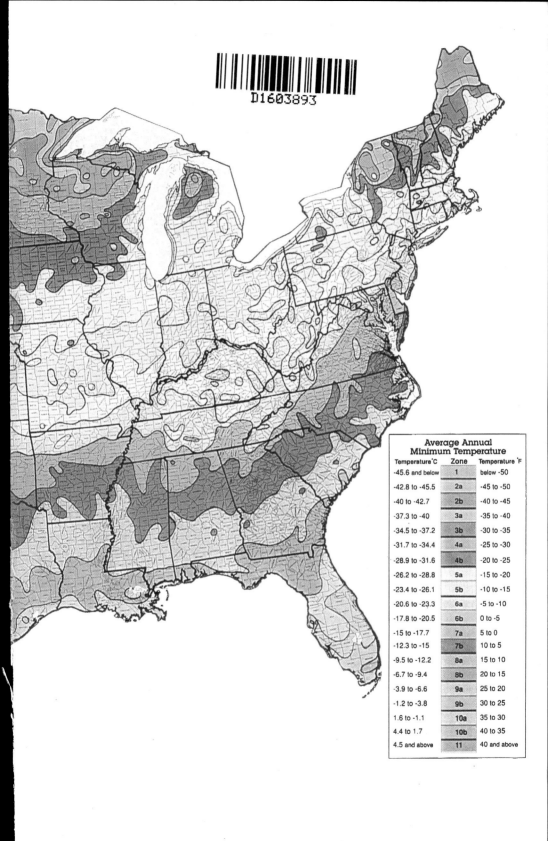

Average Annual
Minimum Temperature

Temperature °C	Zone	Temperature °F
-45.6 and below	1	below -50
-42.8 to -45.5	2a	-45 to -50
-40 to -42.7	2b	-40 to -45
-37.3 to -40	3a	-35 to -40
-34.5 to -37.2	3b	-30 to -35
-31.7 to -34.4	4a	-25 to -30
-28.9 to -31.6	4b	-20 to -25
-26.2 to -28.8	5a	-15 to -20
-23.4 to -26.1	5b	-10 to -15
-20.6 to -23.3	6a	-5 to -10
-17.8 to -20.5	6b	0 to -5
-15 to -17.7	7a	5 to 0
-12.3 to -15	7b	10 to 5
-9.5 to -12.2	8a	15 to 10
-6.7 to -9.4	8b	20 to 15
-3.9 to -6.6	9a	25 to 20
-1.2 to -3.8	9b	30 to 25
1.6 to -1.1	10a	35 to 30
4.4 to 1.7	10b	40 to 35
4.5 and above	11	40 and above

D1603893

Growing Camellias in Cold Climates

William L. Ackerman, Ph.D.

Noble House
Baltimore, Maryland

Growing Camellias in Cold Climates

Library of Congress
Cataloging-in-Publication Data
ISBN 1-56167-716-7

Library of Congress Card Catalog Number:
2001119704

All photographs and drawings by the author except where noted. The photographs on page 111 were taken by Dr. Clifford Parks.

Published by

8019 Belair Road, Suite 10
Baltimore, Maryland 21236

Printed in China

Acknowledgements

First, and foremost, I would like to acknowledge my wife, Kitty's, long-enduring support and patience, not only in recent years during the creation of this book, but over the many previous years while I was totally absorbed in camellia hybridization.

Encouragement to publish this book was also given by a wide range of friends and associates, including nurserymen, hobby gardeners, associate horticulturalists, and plant specialists. Without exception, the emphasis has been for a book that addresses the need for a non-technical guideline of camellia culture in climates long considered unsuitable for their survival.

Special thanks are due to those individuals who contributed, directly or indirectly, to the completion of the text. These include Dr. John L. Creech, who through his extensive plant exploration in Asia, provided much of the basic genetic material used in the early breeding program. To Dr. H. Marc Cathey, former Director of the U.S. National Arboretum, for his pioneering work in establishing the U.S. Plant Hardiness Zone maps. To the late Dr. Donald Egolf, for his continued advice and the sharing his laboratory and greenhouse facilities during the immediate years following my retirement. Also, the late Dr. Frank Santamour, for his advice and encouragement during the early years, and Dr. Margaret Pooler, more recently. Margo Williams, and Susan Benz, research technicians, who assisted in much of the early hybridization work which resulted in the first group of *C. oleifera* hybrids.

Thanks also to various members of the Camellia Society of the Potomac Valley and Pioneer Camellia Society. Through their efforts over many decades of trials, a series of commercial camellia cultivars sufficiently cold hardy to be grown locally was established. Charles and Karen Fairchild shared their expertise in computer programming.

Lastly, indebtedness is expressed to the officials and senior horticulturists at the various arboreta and plant institutions where much of the initial field-testing was performed. These included the American Horticultural Society River Farm, Bernard's Inn Farm, Bon Air Park, Brookside Gardens, Hillwood Grounds & Museum, Londontown Publik House and Gardens, Longwood Gardens, McCrillis Gardens, U.S. National Arboretum and the U.S. Plant Introduction Station.

Table of Contents

CHAPTER V

CHAPTER VI

CHAPTER VII

CHAPTER VIII

CHAPTER IX

APPENDICES

Appendix 3

Appendix 4

INDICES

FOREWORD

My first exposure to Camellia research and hybridization came in 1959 following a transfer to the East Coast from the U.S. Plant Introduction Station in Chico, California. As a Research Pomologist, I worked with such tree fruits and nuts as apricots, cherries, peaches, plums, kiwis, and pistachios. My assignment consisted in evaluating and documenting plant importations from around the World for their commercial potential. In California, we lived in a region where Camellias were taken for granted as one of the many reliable garden ornamentals flourishing everywhere. Yet, my only contact with the genus was a large *Camellia japonica* cultivar 'Brilliant'. This plant was growing in front of the house we rented in Chico.

Soon after arriving at the U.S. Plant Introduction Station at Glenn Dale, Maryland, where I was the Horticulturist in Charge, I became aware of the Station's sizeable Camellia collection, which included 24 species, three related genera, and several hundred cultivar-imports from Japan. These plants were the result of various plant explorations made during the 1950s by Dr. John Creech, my predecessor, at Glenn Dale. By 1959 standards, this species collection alone was a rarity and a plant breeder's dream. Through additional explorations during the next decade, the number of Camellia species was increased from 24 to 33. One should remember that this was before the opening of the Peoples Republic of China to plant exports in the early 1980s, and the flood of new species released to the Western world that followed. My new position involved research and administration. This provided an opportunity to develop a research program utilizing this valuable germ plasm. A further boost to my Camellia involvement came a year later when I began study towards a Ph.D. in Plant Genetics. My advisor at the University of Maryland, Dr. Delbert T. Morgan, Botany Professor, suggested camellias as my thesis project. Thus, camellia research served a dual purpose, partly satisfying both my academic and professional requirements. This led to an involvement in cytogenetics, including chromosome analysis, interspecific and intergeneric hybridization, and tissue and embryo culture.

Once involved, it became a fascinating, and even addictive, undertaking. However, while employed with the USDA, there were many other obligations. Following my retirement, love and obsession with camellias took over. With fewer distractions, it has come to occupy a major portion of my time.

In the years prior to retirement, I gradually re-propagated many of the camellias I had used for breeding at the Glenn Dale Station and established them at my seven and a half acre farm in Ashton, Maryland. Along with greenhouse facilities and a small laboratory, I have been able to continue hybridizing and field-testing camellias much as I had done previously.

At the time I purchased the Ashton property in 1962, I had no idea it was climatically unique for the area. It has proven to be an excellent choice. Temperatures here normally run 10 to 12°F below those reported for the Washington, DC area. This may seem a disadvantage to most gardeners, but it was welcome for testing for cold hardiness. Even so, I find myself frequently looking forward to those colder than normal TEST winters. They, I feel, are necessary for the final analysis and selection of those hybrid seedlings worthy to be named and registered.

INTRODUCTION

There are few ornamentals that have the potential for providing as much aesthetic pleasure as Camellias do throughout the calendar year. There is the beauty and elegance of the many flower forms, and the dark lustrous evergreen foliage is matched by few other shrubs. Camellias are also unique in that they bloom during the bleak days of autumn, winter, and early spring, when many plants are dormant. With a judicial selection of both fall and spring bloomers, now readily available in the nursery trade, one can have blooms from late September to early May with but few interruptions—a total of up to eight months. In addition, one can choose from a wide selection of plant forms ranging from prostrate to columnar, open to dense; and various leaf shapes, variegations, and textures.

If this is true, then why are camellias not more widely grown throughout the Northeast, and in similar climatic zones? Much of this is due to several well-established myths about the plant's lack of hardiness. These have pictured Camellias as closely associated with Southern plantation living. On the contrary, Camellias have the genetic potential, through hybridization and selection, to be sufficiently rugged to compete equally with such ornamentals as Rhododendrons, Azaleas, and Hollies.

Much has been written concerning outstanding camellia cultivars (varieties) and their culture, including planting time, site location, pruning, diseases, insects, propagation and usage. However, the numerous texts and articles available today were written by, and directed towards, those living in the "Camellia Belt" (that area along the East Coast from central Virginia south to Florida, west through

Alabama, Mississippi, Louisiana to Texas. After skipping the arid regions of New Mexico and Arizona, it proceeds up through California along the West Coast to the state of Washington - USDA Zones 9 to 7 (30°F down to 0°F) [-1°C down to –18°C]. This also includes similar favorable climatic zones in Japan, Australia, New Zealand, and southern Europe.

These are valuable texts for growers living in those areas, but can be misleading for gardeners wishing to grow camellias in the northern, colder regions. For example, recommendations such as late fall planting, and planting in locations with a southern exposure, can be disasterous in USDA Zones 7 to 5b (0°F down to –15°F) [-18°C down to –26°C]. As a result, progress for successfully growing camellias in the North has been hampered by the prevailing recommendations of southern authors. In effect, this has further strengthened the myth that camellias are only suitable for the 'deep South'.

The information in *Growing Camellias in Cold Climates* is the result of more than forty years of research, breeding, evaluation, and development of cold hardy camellia cultivars by the author. This book establishes those cultural practices necessary for successfully growing camellias where harsh climatic conditions exist. The Northern gardener should be very careful in choosing which of the many cultivars in the nursery trade to plant in his garden. The majority of the camellias available, until recently, have been selected and named by southern growers from seedlings grown in the South where selection has been based on flower size and quality, not adaptation to severe weather. As such, most are far too tender to withstand winter conditions in the North. In contrast, the new *C. oleifera* hybrids presented in this book, have in their parentage, individuals resulting from a selection process that extended for nearly 5,000 years in China, for their adaptation to adverse climatic conditions.

Growing Camellias for Cold Climates provides the best recommendations for growing camellias north of the "Camellia Belt". The cultivars described are limited to those proven cold hardy over many decades. The information and illustrations on each, are more detailed than those found in most other Camellia books. In-depth-profiles are given, where deemed pertinent, for specific cultivars, from the experiences of those growing them.

Where technical information was felt important, an effort has been made to explain matters in a simple straightforward manner.

Buying the right plant for the right site and in the right season, can be critical for the northern gardener. For the right plant, we furnish a list of those nurseries dealing with hardy varieties to help you choose the best plants for your area. For the right planting location, we have an entire chapter on that subject. For the right season, we discuss the pros and cons of various planting times, along with our recommendations.

The primary purpose of *Growing Camellias in Cold Climates* is to present the advantages (there are some) and the challenges encountered by the northern gardener. These emphasize striking differences as compared to those followed by our southern friends. We believe this book is the first of its kind in its presentation of sensible cultural practices for a broad new northern territory now open to the successful growing of the most beautiful of broad-leaved evergreen shrubs—the camellia.

Those readers who are familiar with lavishly illustrated Camellia books showing huge, showy blooms should not compare them with the hybrids in this book. Those books, emphasize plants producing show quality flowers to be entered in competition for winning prizes in Camellia Society sponsored shows. This book portrays camellias as hardy landscape plants with beautiful, moderate-sized blooms. Also, please keep in mind that those authors had many thousands of registered cultivars available (actually, more than 6,000 domestically and 35,000 internationally) to choose from without concern for their hardiness. The plants and flowers illustrated here are ones which, through several decades of field-testing, have proven successful when grown in colder climates. Sources for these plants are now numerous, as indicated in the section on Sources.

It is our hope that we will open to you a new vista of opportunity in areas previously considered hazardous and impractical for Camellia culture.

CHAPTER I

Camellia, native to the Orient, is the largest genus in the family Theaceae, which also includes *Stewartia, Franklinia, Gordonia, Laplacea, Schima, Tutcheria, Pyrenaria,* and *Yunnanea.* Of these, the first three are probably recognizable to most gardeners. They are, with the exception of *Laplacea,* (native to South America), the only genera native to the Americas. Of the six documented species of *Stewartia*, two are native to eastern North America. *Gordonia* species are represented in both eastern North America and Asia. *Franklinia* is unique in being strictly domestic. Comprised of only one species, *F. alatamaha*, it was first discovered in 1765, growing along the Altamaha River in Georgia by botanist John Bartram and his son William. On a later trip, William brought seeds back to their botanic garden in Philadelphia. It was named in honor of John Bartram's good friend, Benjamin Franklin. The tree was never again seen in the wild after 1803. All the Franklinias growing today are propagations from those original collections by the Bartrams. (Figures 1-1 and 1-2)

We enjoy camellias for their beautiful flowers and as an evergreen landscape plant. However, in its native Orient, it was grown primarily for its utilitarian value. The common tea plant, was originally classified as *Thea sinensis*. Only in 1935 was it redesignated as *Camellia sinensis*. It has been grown in China as a beverage crop since around 2,700 B.C. In China, and later in Japan, tea became the national drink, and today is used in a ritual Tea Ceremony in both countries.

Camellia oleifera, grown as a source of seed oil used in cooking, hair dressing, and cosmetics, has been cultivated for at least as long as tea, if not longer. From an economic viewpoint, these two species (*C. sinensis* and *C. oleifera*), are the most important, and far exceed in value all other species within the genus. Camellias as ornamentals in China and Japan, appear to be closely associated with Buddhist monasteries and Shinto Shrines, where they were highly prized in China by 600 to 900 A.D., and a bit later in Japan. (Figures 1-3 and 1-4)

Our knowledge regarding the number of species within the genus *Camellia* changed dramatically with the opening of China to the West. In the 1920s, there were only 40 recognized species. In 1958, this was increased to 82 documented, and 20 unclassified species, listed in the book *A Revision of the Genus Camellia,* by J. Robert Sealy. This became the Bible of reference during all of the 1960s and much of the 1970s. My own interspecific compatibility studies during those years, closely agreed with Sealy's taxonomic classification and separation of species into twelve sections. By 1984, the number had increased to over 200 species, documented in the book *Camellias* by Chang Hung Ta and Bruce Bartholomew. Since then, with the free access to literature from China, there has been a steady procession of the documentation of new species each year. Exactly where the count stands today is an open question, although reports go as high as 270 species.

Some caution should be exercised in recognizing this last number. I have had a long association with many taxonomists and have learned that they generally are of two distinct philosophies— the 'lumpers' and the 'splitters', depending on how broadly they consider diversity is allowable within a species. Some 'splitters' consider even minute differences as justification for documenting separate new species. I suspect that Chinese taxonomists tend to fall into this latter category.

Within China, the origin of the genus *Camellia* is more specifically located in the south and south western parts of the country. An accepted method of pinpointing a center of origin of a genus is to add up the number of endemic (native) species within an area. The greater the number of species within an area, the

Figure 1-1- *Franklinia alatamaha*, a deciduous shrub hardy to Massachusetts.

Figure 1-2- *Franklinia alatamaha.* Blooms in Maryland from late July to killing frosts.

Figure 1-3- Todaiji Temple, Nara, Japan. **Figure 1-4-** Kusuga Shrine, Nara, Japan.

longer is the history of the evolution of the genus in that area. Using numbers as a criteria, it would appear that in the People's Republic of China, the provinces of Yunnan and Guangxi constitute the origin center of the genus *Camellia*. From there, it spread East into Gaungdong and south into Northern Vietnam. Species diversity decreases significantly from there in all directions (Figure 1-5).

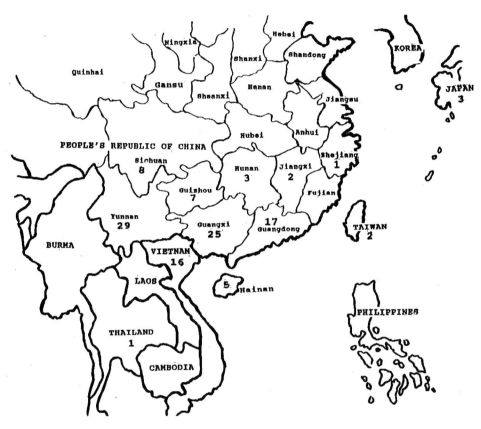

Figure 1-5 - The number of endemic Camellia species within the various provinces of China and the surrounding countries

Camellias in Europe

Europeans first became interested in camellias, not for their ornamental value, but as a source of tea. It is said that the Chinese, unwilling to relinquish their monopoly in the tea trade, gave the early European sea traders plants of such ornamental species as *C. japonica* and *C. reticulata*, instead. A fierce competition developed between the Portuguese, Dutch, and English East Indies Trading companies, throughout the 17th and 18th centuries.

The dates of the earliest importations of camellias into Europe vary widely, depending upon which reports one reads. Transporting live plants half way around the world in those days was extremely difficult. Probably because of this, and the belief that camellia leaves had certain herbal properties, the first dried specimens were sent from China to England between 1700 and 1702, of *C. japonica*, *C. sinensis* (tea plant), and *C. fraterna*. Living camellia plants were brought into Europe from the Orient by the Dutch and Portuguese from about 1730 onwards. Other reports state that the tea plant came to England in the late 16th to early 17th century. All these dates fall by the wayside if one considers a report by Dr. Frederick G. Meyer, U.S. National Arboretum, Washington, DC. During a plant exploration trip through southern Europe in 1957, Dr. Meyer visited Oporto, Portugal, where he became privy to documented evidence that *C. japonica* was first introduced to Europe by the Portuguese, in the first half of the 16th century. Supposedly, three plants of *C. japonica* from Japan were planted in an Oporto garden around 1550.

Camellias in America

As in Europe, the early interest in camellias in America was in the tea plant. In 1744, seeds of *C. sinensis* were introduced to Savannah, Georgia. This first attempt proved a failure, so another attempt was made in 1772. Although this later introduction was successful, tea growing in Georgia did not thrive. Still later in 1813, efforts were made to grow tea in the Charleston, South Carolina area. Tea growing lasted longer there, but eventually also succumbed.

In 1797 *C. japonica* was imported from England to Hoboken, New Jersey. Also during the late 1700s and early 1800s, nurserymen in the Northeast, imported seeds as well as plants of *C. japonica*, from Europe. This resulted in new cultivar names quite distinct from those in Europe. In areas as far north as Boston, camellias became associated with greenhouse culture, for producing flowers popular in the florist trade.

Camellias became ever more popular for outdoor plantings in the South, and greenhouse growing in the North. Both here, and abroad, the interest in camellias peaked in the early 1860s, then went out of favor until well into the 20th century. Whether the Civil War had anything to do with the decline in America is not clear. However, the plants acquired a reputation for being difficult to grow, and for requiring special greenhouse conditions.

There is little agreement as to just when the renewed interest in camellias began. It would seem that it developed slowly during the 1930s and gradually built up from then. Landmark events, perhaps, are good indicators of its progress. The Azalea and Camellia Society of America was started in 1932, with contacts in five states. In 1939, The Camellia Society of America split away from the Azalea group and published its first Yearbook. Finally, in 1946, the Camellia Society of America reorganized to become the present American Camellia Society. Since then, it has waxed and waned periodically. It grew to over 5200 members in 44 states and 18 foreign countries by the late 1970s, having survived a severe drop in interest during the early 1960s. At that time, many organizations, both horticultural and other, also suffered. Again, in the early 1980s, there was a large drop in membership among local camellia societies throughout the mid-Atlantic region. Here, the cause was due, at least in part, to a series of exceptionally severe winters during the late 1970s into the early 1980s, which devastated outdoor camellia plantings. The introduction of more cold hardy hybrids and new techniques for protecting outdoor plants (both factors discussed in detail later) were responsible for an upsurge in interest during the late 1980s and through to the present.

The number of registered cultivars has expanded rapidly during recent decades and is, in itself, an indicator of its popularity. The Southern California Camellia Society, in conjunction with the American Camellia Society, publishes *The Camellia Nomenclature.*

This lists the names, brief descriptions, year of introduction, and originator, of cultivars grown in the United States. Updated every third year, the 23rd Edition, 1999 issue, contains about 6,200 cultivars. In comparison, the two volume *International Camellia Register*(1993) contains more than 35,000 cultivar names. Both of these publications are available through the American Camellia Society.

The reason why tea growing has not been successful in America, is a mystery. The plants grow well in the Southeast, especially in South Carolina. However, harvesting and processing premium quality tea is a high labor intensive procedure and it was apparently difficult to compete with the low cost Oriental labor. As late as 1974, during my years with the USDA Plant Introduction Section, we cooperated with representatives of the Lipton Tea Company and the University of South Carolina, in furnishing tea germplasm from the Orient for trials in test plots at several experimental stations. This entailed a further study of the feasibility of commercial tea production throughout South Carolina. The objective was to use specialized mechanical harvesters deemed adequate for the production of instant tea. Today, there is a viable commercial tea growing business, the American Classic Tea Company, situated on Wadmalaw Island off the coast of South Carolina, which advertises its product as the only tea grown in America. Harvesting is done with modern custom-made machinery, which enables them to produce a very fine quality tea.

Plant Hardiness Map of Europe

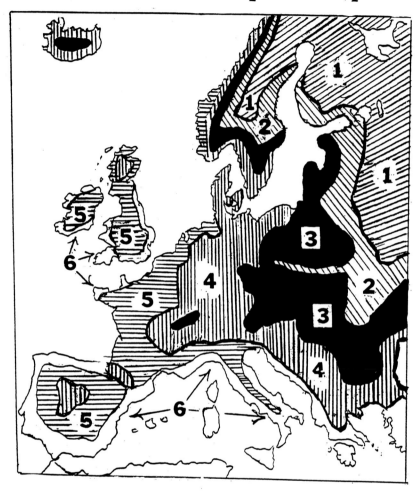

Temperature Zone

1	-30°C & below	4	-12°C to -18°C
2	-22°C to -30°C	5	-6°C to -12°C
3	-18°C to -22°C	6	Above -6°C

CHAPTER II

THE PATH TO GREATER HARDINESS

Many Americans associate Camellias with southern plantations, Magnolias, and perhaps Scarlett O'Hara strolling through lush gardens picking gorgeous blooms for some upcoming ball. This concept has been difficult to change, but in recent years a more realistic picture is gradually coming into focus. The change has come through the persistent efforts of many individuals living outside the "Camellia Belt" (See Introduction) dedicated to extending the cultural range well beyond that previously accepted for this beautiful ornamental.

With the exception of a few early pioneers, it was not until the years immediately after World War II that a renewed interest developed in Camellias as landscape shrubs rather than just greenhouse specimens grown for their show flowers. This has come through a series of activities that have, and continue, to make camellia growers more aware of the full potential within the genus.

Briefly, these consist of:

1. The persistent efforts by a number of growers outside the "Camellia Belt" to select those cultivars best adapted to their climatic conditions and discontinue planting those that do not come up to standard.
2. The establishment of trial gardens utilizing those cultivars which appear most promising.
3. The introduction of new hardier species from the Orient
4. Breeding efforts directed toward greater hardiness

5. Studies about various environmental factors besides freezing temperatures that affect plant survival.

Selecting plants best adapted to one's local climatic conditions is a tradition for plant improvement that goes back to ancient times when man changed from a hunter-gatherer culture to a grower-harvester. Thus, it was only natural that northern gardeners would bring plants from the south for trials in their gardens. This process of selective trials has been taking place for well over half a century, and cultivars better adapted to northern areas were distinguished from their more tender cousins.

It should be mentioned that this discussion deals primarily with plant hardiness, and only secondarily with flower bud hardiness. Flower bud hardiness is of concern mostly with spring blooming types whose buds are exposed all winter and which can be killed during a severe winter. Also, a sudden freeze at the wrong time can wipe out much of a season's blooms. From a southerners viewpoint this may be considered a severe loss. To a Northerner, it does not compare with the heavy winter injury, or death, of plants several decades old.

The most extensive and longest sustained study of flower bud hardiness was done by Wendell M. Levi, of Sumter, SC. His voluminous records and appraisals have been documented in ten separate presentations over a span from 1955 to 1973, in the American Camellia Society yearbooks. Many of Levi's conclusions regarding cold damage to flowers correlate well with later studies of cold damage to plants. He found it necessary to make changes in his numerical ratings of individual cultivars from time to time, either raising or lowering their status based on additional information. Mr. Levi placed the cultivars under evaluation into four classes with Class I composed of those cultivars that bloomed successfully after temperatures as low as 4°F.

Dr. Clifford Parks, broadly defined the parameters of hardiness in *C. japonica* as follows: "In climates which do not experience temperatures below 15°F for long periods, *C. japonica* is fully hardy. Only very tender varieties display symptoms of cold injury to dormant buds when exposed to temperatures of 15°F, or higher, for short periods. Normally, vegetative injury does not occur at these temperatures.

Parks and Doyle (1983) found a strong correlation between plant and flower hardiness patterns during very cold winters in North Carolina, but not in milder ones. The author also found correlations between floral and foliar hardiness with enough exceptions to feel the relationship was not a strong one. However, I did find that among hybrids of *C. oleifera* crossed with *C. vernalis*, blooming in December and early January, both plants and flowers showed exceptional hardiness. Also, *C. oleifera* (PI 162561) appears to transmit increased hardiness to partially-opened flowers, as well as dormant buds.

An early pioneer in the search for greater cold hardiness was Dr. P. W. Zimmerman, Boyce Thompson Institute, Yonkers, New York. In 1927, he obtained Camellia cuttings from the University of Washington, Seattle, Washington. The identity of the material was unavailable, so he labeled it "Variety Z'. This initial material was the incentive to start him on an extensive camellia trial period that was still active at his last report in 1955. Several plants of 'Variety Z' continued to grow in his garden during that entire period. Six separate collections have been mentioned at Boyce Thompson Institute, beginning in 1934. During the ensuing years, Dr. Zimmerman was responsible for introducing into the New York City metropolitan area, named cultivars such as 'Elegans', Kumasaka ,' 'S Frost', 'Madame Lebois', 'Compte de Gomer', among others, for testing outside.

These, and a large number of seedlings, were grown first in the Boyce Thompson greenhouses prior to distribution to private and institute gardens in upper Westchester County, New York, and northern New Jersey. At about this same time, vegetative propagations of 'Variety Z' were sent to the U.S. National Arboretum, Washington, DC. This variety has since become a permanent part of my breeding program.

It is interesting that many of Dr. Zimmerman's observations on the cultural aspects of growing camellias in a harsh climate are remarkably similar to my own independent conclusions. Dr. Zimmerman found that it takes at least two years for camellia plants to become well established after being transplanted outside. It takes even longer if the root system is pot bound. Contrary to popular belief at the time, he found that outdoor camellias send their roots very deep into the ground. Zimmerman also found that those camellias that survived best were ones which had been planted outside when quite small. In this way he felt they were better able to establish themselves in their permanent location. (This subject will be handled in some detail in Chapter III). Zimmerman also found that winter sun seemed to be harmful, at least to the foliage, whereas summer sun (in New York) appeared to do no particular damage.

Unfortunately, no information of further testing by Zimmerman has been available since 1955, fully four years before I first became involved with Camellias. However, his work of testing only *C. japonica* varieties and seedlings was typical for that period. Most studies, until quite recently, were limited to ratings of hardiness within existing cultivars of *C. japonica* and to a lesser extent *C. sasanqua*. There were rarely any efforts towards a systematic breeding program directed to create new hybrids with greater hardiness.

Success has not come without serious setbacks over the years. A good example has been the experiences of camellia growers in the Washington, DC metropolitan area. Many of these camellia enthusiasts were from the South, having moved to the Nation's Capital to serve at Federal Agencies during World War II, and the immediate years afterwards. This, perhaps, provided an advantage in the efforts to expand camellia culture northward. These former southerners were more persistent in their drive to establish camellias locally in their gardens. Also, there was a long period prior to the mid-1970s, when growers lived with the false security brought about by relatively mild winters. During this period, more and more new cultivars were grown successfully.

This all came to an end with back-to-back harsh winters in 1976-77 and 1977-78. Those years separated the men from the boys among camellia cultivars. It was also a time when camellia growers began a realistic search for cultivars capable of surviving in the new harsh climate. Periodic severe winters since have kept us vigilant in our observations.

Active in this study over the years were Milton Brown, Douglas D. Hall, Dr. Arthur Maryott and Bill Miller, all members of the Camellia Society of the Potomac Valley (CSPV), and Dr. C.T. Ling, Emerson Waltz, Zenobia Kendig and John Pumphrey of the Pioneer Camellia Society (PCS) of Baltimore. Suggested cultivar lists were compiled by each Society, which have been subject to periodic revisions during the ensuing years. What began in the early 1960s with a list of well over a hundred cultivars, has been reduced to several dozen spring bloomers and a handful of fall flowering types.

First, let us start our list of survivors with the U.S. National Arboretum planting. From a collection of 956 specimens in the mid-1970s, only the following spring flowering (*C. japonica*) specimens survived to see the 1980s:

Berenice Boddy	Paulette Goddard
C. M. Wilson	Dr. Tinsley
Elegans (Chandleri)	R. L. Wheeler
Governor Mouton	Rev. John C. Drayton
Kumasaka	Tricolor (Siebold) Red
Leucantha	Variety Z

Among the fall flowering there were even fewer specimens remaining:

Agnes O. Solomon (*C. sasanqua*)	Jean May
Showa-no-Sake (*C. hiemalis*)	

At this same time, Dr. C. T. Ling, of Baltimore, Maryland, was compiling a list that included most of these same cultivars plus the following additional spring bloomers:

Blood of China	Herme
Donckelarii	Lady Clare
Eleanor Haygood	Lady Vansittart
Flame	Ville de Nantes

And such fall flowering *C. sasanqua* cultivars as:

Cleopatra   Sharon Elizabeth

During the early 1980s, the two local camellia societies struggled to maintain their existence. Probably the single most important act that saved them was the use of Microfoam (see Chapter IV) as a winter protection insulating material to help the badly injured plants regain their former stature and protect new plantings from damage.

Through a process of frequent surveys and wide membership participation, revised lists of recommended cultivars were compiled by each society: Many of the same varieties were independently selected by the two societies. The combined list is as follows:

C. japonica

Red
Blood of China
Flame
Glen 40
Jarvis Red
Mathotiana
Paulette Goddard
Tricolor (Siebold) Red*
Pink
Berenice Boddy
Dr. Tinsley*
Elegans
Herme
Kumasaka*
Lady Clare*
Pink Perfection

White
Frost Queen*
Leucantha*
Purity*
White Empress
White Queen

Variegated
Donckelarii
Governor Mouton*
Lady Vansittart
Tricolor (Siebold)

*Selected by both the Washington Camellia Society of the Potomac Valley and the Pioneer Camellia Society of Baltimore.

C. sasanqua

Red	White
Yuletide	Setsugekka
Pink	White Edged Pink
Cleopatra	Hana-jiman
Jean May	

C. hiemalis
Kanjiro
Showa-no-sakae

Growing any of these cultivars is no guarantee of its performance. However, on the average, these varieties had a better track record, under varied growing conditions, than other camellias tested in the area, through the mid 1980s. Since then, Bob Hope and Herme, among the spring flowering, and Cleopatra, among fall flowering, have been reclassified as marginal.

Although significant progress has been made utilizing the field-testing of large numbers of existing *C. japonica* and *C. sasanqua* cultivars, this procedure has its limitations. Most of the cultivars under evaluation are chance seedlings of older garden specimens. This suggests a degree of inbreeding with selection based on pleasing flowers, not greater hardiness within a limited gene pool. The best way to break out of this confinement is to conduct hybridization programs directed to the specific objective of increasing cold hardiness. The purpose would be to reshuffle the genes controlling cold-resistance among selected cold hardy parents so that a percentage of the progeny would, hopefully, have more hardiness than either parent. Here, rather than depend upon the chance randomization of the right genes coming together from open pollinated seedlings, controlled crosses would accumulate these genes more directly into specific seedlings.

During the early to mid 1960s, Dr. Clifford Parks, while he was a Geneticist at the Los Angeles State and County Arboretum, Arcadia, CA, embarked on a well-planned breeding program with the specific objective of developing more cold resistant progeny.

During 1962 and 1963, combinations were made between cultivars known to have survived in colder areas. This was expanded in the 1964-66 seasons, with crosses between cultivars surviving in field plantings at Longwood Gardens at Kennett Square, PA.

These hybrid seedlings were subsequently field tested with 23 collaborators at various arboreta and botanic gardens throughout much of the Eastern U.S. from South Carolina to Massachusetts, and west to Missouri. Cuttings were distributed to these collaborators of about 1,000 hybrid seedlings representing 57 different hybrid combinations.

The collaborators then grew these on for the establishment of field trial plantings at each station. This represented the first systematically directed breeding program for the development of a series of cold hardy hybrid progeny suitable for planting in USDA Zones 6b (0° to -5°F). Among the final selections were Park's April Series' including cultivars: 'April Blush', 'April Dawn', 'April Remembered', 'April Rose,' 'April Snow,' and 'April Tryst'.

Dr. Ackerman's hybridization and related work with Camellias beginning in 1959, was conducted at the U.S. Plant Introduction Station, Glenn Dale, Maryland. Although transferred to the U.S. National Arboretum in 1974, his laboratory, greenhouse and field facilities remained at Glenn Dale. From that time until his retirement, he commuted between the two facilities on a regular basis. Since the Glenn Dale Station is little known outside the Department of Agriculture, a brief history, description, and outline of its functions, follows.

The U.S. Plant Introduction Station, located on a 70-acre site about 16 miles northeast of Washington, DC, was established in 1919 by the U.S. Department of Agriculture. Its purpose has been testing plants of potential economic benefit to the United States. One of four Federal introduction gardens across the country, the Glenn Dale station, in its function as the 'Ellis Island' for plant imports, received an enormous range of plant species from around the world. As such, it served as the primary source of seeds, plants, cuttings, and related material, for use by university scientists, agriculturists, and growers. For nearly all its history, this Station was the center of Plant Quarantine facilities for the entire

Department of Agriculture, and the most highly developed of the four stations. Its location is convenient to the Beltsville, Maryland Agriculture Department Headquarters, and the Plant Quarantine Inspection House. With the construction of a state-of-the-art plant quarantine facility at Beltsville, the Agricultural Research Service transferred many of the activities from Glenn Dale to Beltsville. Beginning in the late 1980s, the U.S. National Arboretum gradually took over the grounds at Glenn Dale, as Plant Quarantine was phased out. Today, the Arboretum is the sole occupant, with the Glenn Dale Station serving as one its satellite facilities.

Among plant specimens at the Station, it maintained the most comprehensive species collection of camellias and related genera, outside of Asia, until the recent opening of the Peoples Republic of China to Western plant exploration. This original collection became the germ plasm foundation for the breeding program begun by the Author in 1959. During the early to mid 1960s, Dr. Ackerman was involved in propagating and field-testing camellia introductions from Asia. Many of these had been collected by Dr. J. L. Creech, U.S.D.A. Plant Explorer, and also, separately, through foreign seed and plant exchange. The collections of Dr. Creech involved a wide climatic range in Japan, including mountainous regions near the West Coast, and at Aomori, the northern-most regions of wild camellias.

These introductions had little commercial possibilities in themselves, and the early studies were directed towards screening for the most cold resistant to be used as potential breeding parents for subsequent generations.

Also at that time, Ackerman conducted a rather extensive compatability study within the family *Theacae*, including Camellia. This involved reciprocal interspecific crosses, including *C. oleifera* with *C. sasanqua*, *C. hiemalis*, *C. vernalis*, and others. It was only later after discovering the superiority of the *C. oleifera* hybrids in field tests over other selections, that the true value of *C. oleifera* was realized. The 1969 *C. oleifera* crosses resulted in the naming of 'Frost Prince' and 'Frost Princess', the forerunners of many other *C. oleifera* hybrids to follow.

The winter devastation experienced during the late 1970s, as described previously, emphasized both the urgent need for greater cold resistance and the value of *C. oleifera* as a breeding parent. It was soon discovered that not all *C. oleifera* strains are cold tolerant. Eight separate Asian introductions were tested and only two - Plant Introduction (P.I.) 162475, later named 'Lu Shan Snow', and P.I. 162561, proved truly cold hardy.

Camellia oleifera, as mentioned in Chapter I, has been widely grown in China for close to 5,000 years. As a source of edible seed oils, it was, and continues to be, prized as a valuable crop. Over the centuries, efforts were made to extend its culture into ever-wider areas. This species is presently grown in China over an area encompassing 9.74 million acres (15,238 square miles). This is closely equivalent to the combined land areas of the states of Maryland and Connecticut. Some of these areas were much colder than that considered normal, for camellias. Where it occasionally was successful, local hardy strains developed. We have been fortunate, to have introduced, by chance, two such strains. (Figures 2-1, 2-2, 2-3, and 2-4).

Between 1979 and 1981, 2,500 inter-specific hybrids were made, using *C. oleifera* strains P.I. 162475 and P.I. 162561, crossed with various *C. sasangua*, *C. hiemalis*, and *C. vernalis* cultivars. In addition, a series of *C. oleifera* x *C. sasanqua* hybrids developed in 1969 were back-crossed to *C. oleifera*. This has continued each year since, with lesser numbers of hybrid progeny.

The hybrids were greenhouse grown for two years, and then planted out for field testing at 14 locations, mostly institutions and arboreta, in eastern Pennsylvania, northern Maryland, northern Virginia, and western North Carolina. A second series of crosses made between 1980 and 1984 resulted in more *C. oleifera* hybrids. This time, however, spring-flowering parents, including *C. japonica*, and *C. X Williamsii* were used.

Field evaluation surveys were begun in 1982 and have continued to the present. During this time, the test locations have experienced repeated sub-zero minimum temperatures extending to −15°F, once in 1985, and again in 1994. Periodic evaluation, over the years, entailed considerable travel by the Author. As promising individuals were identified, scions were taken for

Figure 2-1- *C. oleifera* **'Lu Shan Snow'** (PI 162475) 24' high and 30' wide.

Figure 2-2- *C. oleifera* **'Lu Shan Snow'.** Powdery cinnamon-colored trunks.

Figure 2-3- *C. oleifera* **'Lu Shan Snow'** Blooms from October to November.

Figure 2-4- *C. oleifera* (PI162561). Most cold hardy of all camellias tested.

propagation at Ashton, Maryland, where they would be under closer observation. Absence of winter injury was the primary selecting factor. However, this was closely followed by commercial acceptability of the flowers, involving size, quality, and substance, as well as plant form and growth habit. As a result, a series of new cultivars continue to be released, including both fall and spring-flowering types. A listing of these, with descriptions, is given in Chapter VIII.

The accepted northern limits for successfully growing camellias in the Eastern U.S., has fluctuated widely during the past 50 years. For the years up to the late 1970s, it was considered relatively safe north as far as the Washington, DC area, southern Maryland, most of Delaware, and parts of Long Island, NY. By the early 1980s, following a series of severe winters, this 'safe' zone moved south to the Norfolk, VA area. By the early 1990s, the zone had returned to its former boundaries.

With the introduction of the *C. oleifera* hybrids, there has been another northern movement into coastal New England, including Massachusetts, as well as sporadically in some mid-western states bordering the southern fringes of the Great Lakes.

Several nurserymen, distributors of the *C. oleifera* hybrids, have provided us with information outlining the more extreme climatic regions from which they receive customers and retail sales requests. A number of these people have written to us directly about various aspects of growing camellias under adverse conditions. Also, we maintain correspondence with growers in northern Europe. This by no means indicates these areas should be considered 'safe' for growing camellias. It does illustrate that many gardeners are anxious to grow camellias regardless of the obvious climatic hazards involved.

U.S. Plant Introduction Station
Glenn Dale, MD

Camellia Hybrid Seedlings
growing at Glenn Dale, in
preparation for field testing

Third year field testing at
Ashton, MD

Fifteen-year-old hybrid
Camellias at Ashton, MD

U.S. National Arboretum
Washington, DC

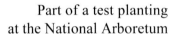
Part of a test planting
at the National Arboretum

Part of a test planting at River Farm
Mount Vernon, VA

Part of a test planting at
Londontown Publik House
and Gardens, Edgewater, MD

Camellias growing on
property of Mrs. Polly
Hill, Martha's Vineyard,
Massachusetts
(photo by Polly Hill)

"Kumasaka" growing on
property of Nickolas
Nickou, MD, Branford,
Connecticut
(photo by Dr. Nickou)

"Bette Sette" growing on property of Mrs. M. Dragan Toronto, Canada (photo by Mrs. Dragan)

"Blood of China" growing on property of Dr. Arthur Maryott, Bethesda, Maryland (photo by Dr. Maryott)

CHAPTER III

Much of what has been written about Camellia culture pertains to their growth and development in the so-called 'Camellia Belt'. These recommendations, although widely accepted, are NOT suitable for growing camellias in colder climates. In many cases, utilizing these cultural procedures can prove disastrous if followed in the North.

One of the primary goals of this book is to point out these differences and to direct northern camellia growers in a direction that will provide them with success.

Factors Affecting Plant Survival

Freezing temperatures are the universal criteria for judging both flower and plant hardiness. This is because we do not have a better single measurement upon which to make determinations. Actually, the situation is more complex than that of mere degrees of coldness. This is why the same cultivar may show wide variations in physical damage from similar minimum temperatures in different locations, or the same plant in different seasons. Methods of plant culture can, in themselves, be of considerable influence on the plant's general health and ability to withstand adverse climatic conditions. Flower and plant damage attributed to freezing temperatures, may actually have been influenced by other factors. Frequently, winter injury is used as a 'cultural catchall' for other forms of damage.

What are some of these contributing factors? In addition to its genetic makeup, a camellia plant's ability to survive sub-freezing temperatures with minimal flower and foliage damage depends on a series of physiological and environmental conditions. A partial list would include:

1. How well established the plant's root system is at its present location.
2. The degree of dormancy.
3. Protection from drying winds.
4. Exposure to early morning winter sun.
5. Presence or absence of filtered shade.
6. Air drainage.
7. Soil moisture retention.
8. Soil color and texture.
9. Duration of low temperature and the prior 72-hour temperatures.
10. Mechanical injury from cultivating and/or mowing equipment.
11. Fertilization program.
12. Plants on their own roots versus grafted plants.
13. Previous year's pruning.
14. Abundance of flowering prior to freeze.
15. Abundance or absence of ground cover or mulch.
16. Possible exposure to rabbit, field mice/vole damage.

Most container plants, including camellias, sold in the nursery trade, are out of balance regarding the ratio of top growth to their root systems. For example, a three-gallon plant (a popular size for planting out) will average 2-1/2 to 3 feet in height. Such a plant may thrive under normal nursery conditions where it is given close attention and receives regular watering and fertilizing. However, in the landscape it will continue to need similar attention throughout its first year. A well-established root system is essential for a healthy stress-resistant plant.

Optimum Season for Planting

Planting camellias in the fall in Maryland and northward (a frequent practice) is a chancy business at best. If the first winter is a mild one, you may succeed, if not, it can cause the death of the plant. Soils can cool rapidly after mid-September and new root development is usually minimal. Yet, every Camellia book I have read (written exclusively by authors living in mild climates), recommends fall planting. A popular time in the south is at the time of leaf fall of the local deciduous trees. The logic here is to allow the plants to get established during the anticipated mild winter in preparation for the stress of the southern hot summer that will follow. **This is absolutely the worst time of the year for northern camellia growers**. In contrast, they need to rely on the relatively mild summers to prepare the plants for the stress of their first winter. Unfortunately, some northern nurserymen further this concept by promoting the fall flowering cultivars while they are in bloom and most salable. This problem could be moderated if they cautioned their customers about providing winter protection the first winter.

We, in the North, have recommended spring planting for many years, preferable between mid April and late May. We also recommend using Microfoam (or burlap) shields around camellia plants the first winter. (This will be discussed in detail in Chapter IV).

Planting a severely root-bound plant without special preparation is inviting trouble. If the roots circle the inside of the container, they need to be gently loosened and spread out in the planting hole. I have dug plants, including camellias, which had been in the ground for several years where the pot bound roots had never ventured beyond their former position. Similarly, if the planting hole is filled with straight compost, sometimes a barrier can form between it and the native soil discouraging the spread of the roots. I always mix the native soil with any organic matter, such as compost, that is added to the hole (do not use peat moss). These are all factors that can influence the survival of plants.

One inspiring trait of camellias is their unique ability to rebound after a bad winter! Never give up hope! Many camellias will sprout from the trunk as late as June after a bad winter. By the end of the second or third season, they will have regained much of their former size and vigor. A true resurrection!

The degree of plant dormancy directly before a sudden drop to sub-freezing temperatures can make a life or death difference. More a problem in the South, we are also susceptible in Maryland and northward. During the second week of January 1985, we had low to mid 50s, followed by -10^0F in the third week of the month. Plants with southern exposures had more leaf burn than a comparable group of cultivars in northern shade. Apparently, the first group had begun to lose some of their dormancy. These same plants had been subjected to comparable low temperatures in previous winters without injury. It has been found that the 72 hours prior to a severe drop in temperature can be most critical.

Plant dormancy is also influenced by the use of high nitrogen fertilizer late in the season. Studies with fruit trees have indicated that low nitrogen, and high potassium and phosphorus, can decrease winter injury by increasing the soluble salt content of plant cell sap. One does wonder whether there is a relationship between this phenomenon and the observation that often individual heavily blooming branches on fall flowering varieties tend to be more severely winter-damaged than their sparse blooming companions. Could the drain on plant nutrients in that branch make it more vulnerable?

The greater susceptibility of some grafted plants to winter injury compared to those grown on their own roots, may depend upon the degree of compatibility between stock and scion. Any graft union that tends to inhibit the free flow of nutrients and water between the plants roots and top, may be less capable of withstanding environmental stress.

Similarly, a plant's ability to replace water lost from transpiration can have a direct effect on its capacity to withstand stress. Light sandy soils have a limited capacity to hold moisture, while heavy clay soils can reduce root development. Neither condition is conducive to healthy plant growth. Also, the amount and frequency of watering can be very important. Less frequent, but thorough, watering encourages deep root development, while frequent light watering increases shallow rooting. Naturally, the latter will be less capable of dealing with environmental stress than for former.

In examining various environmental conditions, one should be aware of possible interactions between two or more factors. Any one by itself may not be particularly harmful but where two or more occur together, they can be deadly. Perhaps a good example was the devastation of the U.S. National Arboretum's camellia collection during the late 1970s, when it was reduced from 956 specimens to slightly more than a dozen struggling individuals. In retrospect, it was probably caused as much by the plants being weakened by the interaction of a least three factors which worked together to create the destruction, rather than the –2°F minimum temperature itself, namely:

1. Droughts during the growing season become evident to every gardener, but those in winter are less obvious. Yet, the November through January period during 1976-77, had only 3.86 inches of rain, while the ten-year normal for that period was 10.55 inches. This had been preceeded by a dryer than usual summer.
2. Excessive drying winds. The low precipitation was accompanied by low humidity that intensified the wind damage.
3. Prolonged temperatures below the freezing point created continuously frozen ground for much of the winter.

Factors 1 and 2 caused high moisture loss while Factor 3 prevented the plants from readily renewing this loss. The result was severe dehydration and death. Many specimens of these same cultivars grown elsewhere experienced lower minimum temperatures without injury.

A number of other such incidents come to mind, but I will use only two for illustration. In my Ashton garden, three plants of 'Winter's Rose' on their own roots, ranging in age from 4 to 12 years, survived –15°F with less than 10% leaf damage. On the other hand, fifty feet away, a two-year old 'Winter's Rose' grafted on *C. oleifera* rootstock was killed to the ground. Similarly, a 'Winter's Rose' planted in October 1993 at the National Arboretum, succumbed that winter at −4°F. Undoubtedly, factors other than minimum temperature were involved. The immediate suspect in the first case would be a restrictive graft union, and in the second, simply not enough time for the plant to become adequately established. In both cases, this is probably an over-simplication.

The second illustration involves a severe ice storm in January 1994 that covered the area with 4" of solid ice. A ten-year old plant of 'Winter's Interlude' situated on a south-eastern slope experienced −15°F with less than 5% leaf damage. Because of its exposure, the ground ice lasted less than a week. A second plant of the same variety (same age) in a more shaded northern location, was killed to the ground. Here, the ice persisted for almost six weeks. A band of similarly sun-sheltered camellias were either severely injured or killed. My wife, Kitty, appropriately named this area 'Death Valley.' Examination of the roots the following spring showed extensive damage. It would appear they died of lack of oxygen in the soil. The bizarre situation here is that the southeastern exposure, normally considered an undesirable location, turned out to be ideal for these unusual weather conditions, while the more traditional shady location proved fatal. Interacting local conditions can affect a plant's ability to survive. It is sometimes difficult to ascertain which factors play the most important function in either enhancing or diminishing a plant's ability to overcome a stressful environment.

These few examples illustrate some of the complications in judging cold hardiness and why evaluating camellias for their winter hardiness can become a long-time project. No single winter's results can be trusted to provide an accurate determination of a cultivar's potential. It is only after many years of testing under a wide range of environmental conditions, that some degree of accuracy can be assured. Thus, the National Arboretum's cold hardy *C. oleifera* hybrid selections were made from over 2,500 seedlings grown at 14 locations in four states, and evaluated over

20 years. Likewise, lists of varieties compiled by members of the Camellia Society of the Potomac Valley (CSPV) and the Pioneer Camellia Society (PCS) of Baltimore, Maryland, were made according to their ability to survive over 20 years of local climatic conditions. Their adaptation is reasonably assured, under most winter conditions.

Site Selection and Microclimates

Camellias in their native Oriental regions are shrubs or small trees, growing among larger trees that offer an over-story of partial protection from sun, wind, and the general elements. Thus, they do best in filtered shade, preferably from needle-leafed evergreens, and less so from large deciduous trees. The leaves, especially of the spring flowering *C. japonica* types, tend towards overall yellowing if exposed to full sun for extended hours each day. On-the-other-hand, there is a direct relationship between the amount of shade and flowering. The more dense the shade, the less the flowering, even though the plants may thrive.

In Northern areas, it is generally accepted that exposure to **very early morning winter sun** can be detrimental to plant health by causing leaf burn, or even plant death. The rationale here is that when the surrounding temperature is well below freezing, the sun shining on dark green foliage can create a microclimate over the leaf surface that is as much as ten to fifteen degrees above that of the surrounding air. With the low relative humidity that frequently exists during cold winter mornings, moisture is drawn out of the leaves creating desiccation. If the ground is frozen, the plant cannot readily replenish this moisture from the root system. Thus, under extreme conditions, the foliage will turn a pale greenish white and become as brittle as corn flakes. Basically, nature has created conditions similar to what we know as 'freeze drying.' As a result, the leaves are killed and the plant will suffer partial or complete defoliation. The solution here is to provide some shade protection during the winter months.

In selecting a suitable site for a new planting, the gardener will undoubtedly need to make compromises. Few of us are blessed with an ideal location. We need to make the best choices from the various sites and exposures available to us. However, in some cases we can overcome local problems through the use of strategically placed fences, hedges and/or 'wind-breaks'. Following is a general description of those characteristics one should strive for, and those that should be avoided, if possible.

Contrary to popular opinion, the best location for camellias in Northern regions is a north, or northwestern, exposure with protection from the prevailing winds. This can be accomplished through shielding by one or more buildings, a substantial wall, or a conifer hedge (example: fast growing Leyland cypress). Here, the plants will hopefully go into a state of dormancy in the autumn and tend to stay that way. Plants exposed to wide fluctuations in temperature do not reach their optimum potential dormancy. It is the sudden change to sub-freezing weather that can be devastating.

Where there is a slope, plant at the TOP, not the bottom, of the incline. Also, avoid a low frost pocket where the surrounding ground on all sides is higher. On still nights, cold air, being heavier than warm air, flows downhill, like water, and accumulates wherever it is obstructed from its downward movement, be it a wall, building, or compact evergreen hedge. I once observed frost damage in a peach orchard while it was in full bloom, and where the rows contoured along the slope. Blooms on the lower rows of trees were all killed up to a middle row where the blooms on the lower half of each tree were killed. However, blossoms on the upper half of those trees and on the trees up the slope were uninjured.

Soils and Mulches

Camellias prefer a well-drained, slightly acid soil (from a pH of 5.5 to 7.0), and will tolerate more acid conditions, but go into a slow decline under alkaline soils. The soils around newly constructed buildings or near new concrete sidewalks, walls, driveways or patios, can produce high lime runoff causing decline and/or death, of nearby camellias. Another associated pH problem in some areas of the country is the prevalence of high alkaline waters.

Although not heavy feeders, camellias do best in soils rich in organic matter and with available slow release nutrients, such as composted leaf mulch. Soil texture can vary from light sandy loam, basic loam, to moderate, but not heavy, clay. Heavy clays, because of the fineness of their particle sizes, provide poor soil aeration. If one is confronted with a heavy clay soil, this can be partially corrected by applying gypsum and organic matter, such as composted pine bark, to increase better water penetration and aeration. Also, planting in raised beds where a good, composted soil is brought in, can alleviate the problem of clay soils.

Moisture

Water, of course, is essential to all living organisms. Many of a plant's requirements are within the control of the gardener. Regular watering is essential to supplement rainfall, especially where the latter is deficient. However, moderation is also important. The old saying of 'too much of even a good thing is too much,' is appropriate. Like most plants, camellias depend upon air spaces between the soil particles as well as moisture. When those spaces become completely filled, it creates a waterlogged condition. With little or no aeration, the roots begin to die. The heavier the soil, the more likely this condition will develop. Camellias are reasonably tolerant of dry conditions after they become well established, considerably more so than azaleas, for example. Actually, camellias would be far more adaptable to adverse conditions, such as drought tolerance and cold hardiness, if it were not for the standard 'southern' method of culture and propagation.

By nature, camellias are tap-rooted plants. Upon germination, most camellia seeds will produce a central root as much as six to eight inches long before producing a stem an inch long. By the time the first true leaves unfold, the root can be more than twelve inches long (Figure 3-1). It is standard policy in the nursery business, to pinch off the root tip, usually at ½ to 5/8 inches, to encourage a branching root system suitable for container culture. This practice is essential for development of the spreading root system desired for pot grown plants. Where this is not done, the

Figure 3-1 - Young Camellia seedlings showing the long taproot in relation to the shoot growth

taproot quickly grows down to the bottom of the container, flattens out and begins to grow in a circular fashion around the bottom of the pot. In severe cases, the primary root may actually strangle itself in its own tight convolutions. The result is a stunted plant, which even when given root freedom, rarely grows properly. Thus, there can be little dispute that the technique of breaking the taproot is a good one for CONTAINER grown plants. However, this compromises the plant's natural means of adaptation to adverse climatic conditions. More about this will be discussed in Chapter IV – Special Situations.

Fertilization

As stated previously, camellias are not heavy feeders and there are probably more cases of adverse effects because of over-fertilization, than for under-fertilization. This is especially true for growing camellias outdoors in Northern climates. The amount of inorganic fertilizer needed largely depends upon soil type. A light sandy loam would need more added amounts of compost and fertilizer than a loam high in organic matter.

Fertilizers, especially those high in nitrogen, stimulate growth. If applied late in the season, it can delay winter dormancy. This is fine in the South where growers welcome vigorous growth and an extended season. However, northern growers would be wise to strive for healthy, slow-growing plants that go into dormancy well before the onset of freezing weather.

Fertilization soon after the end of the spring blooming season should provide sufficient nutrition for the plant until the next year. Fertilizing after the end of June can be risky. A three-month, slow release fertilizer such as, Osmocote 6-18-16, applied in late March or early April is what is frequently recommended for the Northeast.

Pruning

Pruning camellias should be limited to removing diseased or injured branches, undesirable weak growth and, some general shaping involving removal of undesirable wild growth. This is best done in early spring before new growth begins, because pruning, like fertilizing, can stimulate new growth and delay dormancy.

Drastic pruning may, at times, become necessary when transplanting a large specimen. If done properly, even sizeable plants (up to ten feet or more) may be moved safely, especially if planned in advance. One system involves root pruning a year ahead of actual moving. In the spring, one takes a long-bladed spade and cuts down a foot or more around the branch drip line. Cutting the roots stimulates the plant to produce new feeder roots making for somewhat less of a shock in transplanting. The amount of top pruning necessary at the time of transplanting will depend upon how severely the root system has been reduced.

In the nursery trade, young greenhouse grown plants in containers are frequently tip pruned in late fall to create bushy, well-shaped plants. This may be done for the first several years until the plant is offered for sale. It is also a convenient way for the nurseryman to acquire a supply of cuttings for propagation, as well as achieve a sturdy, well-shaped specimen.

SUMMARY FOR GROWING CAMELLIAS
IN NORTHERN CLIMATES

Camellias do best when planted on the **NORTH or WEST** side of a building, provided there is some protection from drying WINTER WINDS.

AVOID FULL SUN, especially early morning sun, during freezing winter weather. This may cause desiccation (like freeze drying). An over-story of EVERGREEN SHADE TREES, (such as PINE), which provide shade all winter, is ideal. Large deciduous trees (such as Oak), can serve as a partial substitute.

SPRING PLANTING is RECOMMENDED, rather than Fall planting, unless the plants are protected the first winter or two. It is less hazardous in our Northern climates, if the roots have a full season to become well established before the onset of winter. **WATER WELL** all season, especially if the weather is dry.

Camellias prefer a slightly **ACID**, well-drained soil, similar to azaleas and rhododendrons.

DO NOT PLANT TOO DEEP! The top of the soil in the container should be level, or slightly above, surrounding ground. Use a **MULCH** of pine needles, non-packing leaves, or pine bark, etc., to a depth of 3-4 inches.

Soil amendments may be well-rotted compost or well composted pine bark.. Use peat moss sparingly, if at all, in the mix, since it becomes too dense with time. Camellias are NOT heavy feeders. A little HOLLYTONE, 5-10-10 fertilizer, or OSMOCOTE 6-18-16, ONCE A YEAR in the SPRING, is sufficient. **DO NOT FERTILIZE AFTER JUNE.**

Newly planted hardy camellias may need some **COLD WEATHER PROTECTION** during their first winter or two. Regular commercial spring blooming cultivars of questionable hardiness, should be covered for several years, and even later, to protect the flower buds from freezing. As a wind and sun screen, a circle of stakes around the plant wrapped with burlap and heavily mulched with dry oak leaves, may be helpful. A **MICROFOAM** blanket (no leaves necessary) is even better. Microfoam is becoming available at some nursery and garden centers.

DEER LOVE TENDER CAMELLIA LEAVES! If you have a problem, fence the small plants, or cover with black netting the first year or so.

CHAPTER IV

A. <u>Winter Protection Structures</u>

As mentioned in Chapter III, it is sometimes helpful to provide extra protection to newly planted camellias during their first winter or two. After that, they should have gotten their roots down and become well enough established in their permanent outdoor location. The primary purpose is to provide protection from drying winds and to modify rapid temperature changes, especially abrupt drops to below freezing. Separate types of structures are normally used for container grown plants that differ from those for individual ground-grown specimens.

Burlap or heavy blankets have been used as insulation for many years. However, in the Washington, DC and Baltimore, Maryland areas, **Microfoam** (DuPont Co., Inc, trade name) has been found more satisfactory. Its use was first brought to the attention of members of the Camellia Society of the Potomac Valley in 1979 by Dr. Francis Gouin, Professor of Horticulture, University of Maryland. Dr. Gouin's original research with Microfoam was in response to requests from nurserymen for a means of protecting their container-grown plants over winter. It was quickly adopted by camellia growers in the area, first for container plants, and then for individual plants grown in the ground.

Microfoam, composed of a sponge-like plastic, used in industrial packing insulation, and comes in 1/4 inch and 3/8 inch thick sheets. The 1/4 inch thickness (the 3/8 inch is rarely used for camellias), allows penetration of sufficient light, yet provides ample insulation to protect camellias from most freezing temperatures. It is usually sold in rolls six feet wide and 225 feet long. Such quantities are more than the average grower requires. To alleviate this problem, our local Camellia Societies purchase in bulk and sell portions at cost to their members. It is also available in smaller quantities at a number of nurseries and garden centers.

One drawback is that Microfoam gradually deteriorates from ultraviolet radiation and, depending on the amount of sun exposure, may need to be replaced after three to five years.

B. Protecting Container Plants

A bare piece of ground, in a shady location with filtered sunlight, is preferred. It should be large enough to accommodate the container plants to be protected. It would be best if the area is slightly mounded, or sloping, to allow adequate drainage. A shallow depression around the perimeter is helpful. If the ground is dry, it should be watered a day or two before the plants are set in place. In Maryland, this is usually done in late November, but it is dependent upon local weather conditions. A reasonable time is after several light frosts, but before a severe one. The first one or two rows of containers are set with the plant tops pointing towards the center of the mound. The rest of the plants are then packed in tight rows facing the first two rows. The top edge of each container should rest on the bottom of the container in the previous row. The plants and surrounding area, are then lightly watered.

A layer of clear plastic is placed over the plants to protect the Microfoam from tears. Next, cover the area completely with a layer of 1/4inch Microfoam that is at least long and wide enough to reach the ground and lay out on the soil surface 6-12 inches. If wider strips of Microfoam are needed to cover the area, it may be necessary to lay two sheets side by side with about a foot overlap and taped together with wide masking tape. Over this is placed another layer of plastic slightly larger than the Microfoam. Essentially then, the Microfoam is sandwiched between two layers of plastic.

If the area is subject to more than several hours of sun daily, the top layer may be covered with either white plastic or clear plastic painted with white latex paint - 1 part paint to 7 parts water. An alternate is some form of shade cloth to cut down the sunlight.

Soil, stones, boards, etc. are placed around the edges of the layers where they rest on the soil. Pine needles, leaves, or straw may also be laid around the edges for extra insulation protection and sealing (see Figure 4-1).

As 'the blanket' traps moisture over the already damp soil, the plants will probably not need to be watered during the winter, but it is good to check them occasionally. If there is a mouse problem locally, it may be well to place poison bait inside the mound before sealing.

The coverings may be gradually removed, starting about the first to the middle of March, depending upon the weather. Since the plants have spent much of their time over winter at relatively high humidity, it is well to uncover them gradually over a period of a week or more to avoid unnecessary shock. Even then, the plants should not be put in an upright position for several more days (preferably on a cool cloudy day without wind). It is not unusual that the plants will be in various stages of flower bud development. Plants with flower buds showing color may be brought into a basement or cool sun porch where temperatures do not exceed 65 degrees. Here, they should flower within a week or two.

C. Protecting Ground Grown Plants

Various methods may be used to protect plants in the ground. These involve some kind of support (stakes or sturdy wire), since the covering, whether of Microfoam, burlap, or blanket, will not stand alone. The structure should be strong enough so it will not collapse under heavy snow. Also, it should be sufficiently anchored to prevent it from being blown away in strong winds.

A simple support can consist of three stakes driven into the ground around the plant so that the Microfoam (or other) covering will not be against any of the branches. A more sturdy system would be to make a cylinder to enclose the plant using utility or

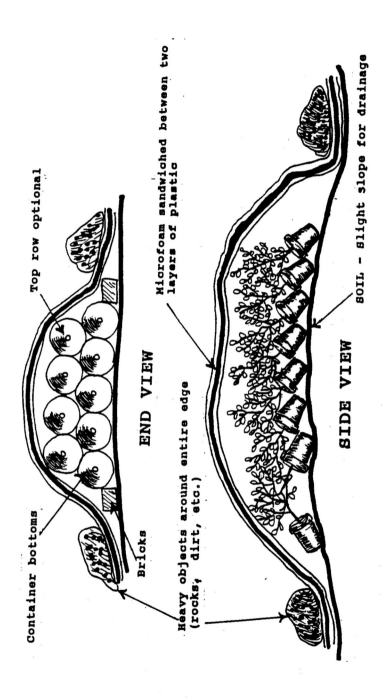

Top row optional

Container bottoms

Bricks

END VIEW

Microfoam sandwiched between two layers of plastic

Heavy objects around entire edge (rocks, dirt, etc.)

SIDE VIEW

SOIL – slight slope for drainage

Fig. 4-1 – Winter Protection of container Camellias using Microfoam

-42-

livestock fencing malleable enough to be bent and yet sturdy enough not to sag. Chicken wire is too fragile.

The Microfoam is cut large enough to encircle the outside perimeter of the wire cylinder with at least several inches overlap. It can be secured with several rounds of twine to hold it in place. The Microfoam is then folded over the top to form a dome and the upper edges clamped together with a series of wooden clothespins. A further precaution against strong winds blowing the covering over is to drive stakes on opposite sides of the cylinder and stretch a line of twine over the top and tie it down firmly (see Figure 4-2).

It is probably well to have the container plants under their protective blanket before hard freezes that may damage their roots (the most vulnerable part of the plant). On the other hand, if the weather permits, plants in the ground should be allowed to harden off several weeks before being put under their winter protection. The actual dates involved will depend upon the prevailing weather in your area. The alert camellia grower should keep aware of daily weather reports as the winter season approaches.

D. <u>A Natural Phenomenon for Conserving Leaf Moisture</u>

We are all aware that, if a plant is not properly watered during a hot summer, it will begin to wilt. Plants continually transpire moisture from their leaves – the amount depending upon temperature and the relative humidity. For any given leaf, the higher the temperature and the lower the humidity, the greater the water loss. Simple, right? During the wintertime the same thing happens, although it is not quite so obvious. The relative humidity some winter days may be comparable to a desert. Any plant that, for an extended period of time cannot maintain a balance between the amount of moisture absorbed, usually through the roots, to that lost through transpiration, is going to die. To survive, a plant must either take in more water, or lose less.

Many camellia growers also grow Rhododendrons. There is a well-recognized phenomenon very characteristic of Rhododendron leaves, where when the plants are subjected to sub-freezing temperatures, the leaves curl upon themselves along the midrib to

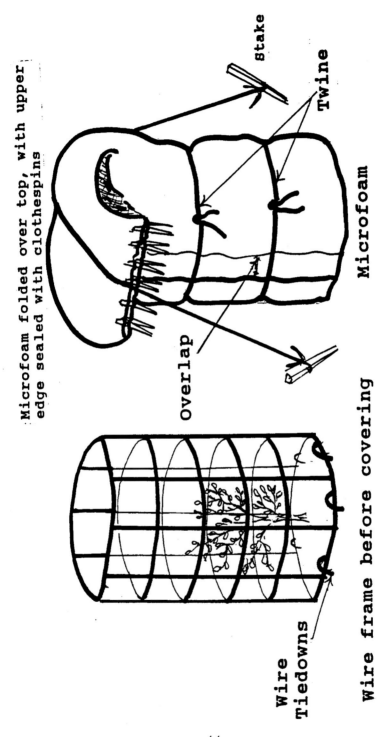

Microfoam folded over top, with upper edge sealed with clothespins

stake

Twine

Microfoam

overlap

Wire frame before covering

Wire Tiedowns

Fig. 4-2 – Winter Protection of ground grown Camellias with Microfoam

-44-

form tube-like structures. The lower the temperature, the tighter they will curl until they may be the diameter of a pencil (see Figure 4-3). When temperatures return to above freezing, the leaves quickly flatten out to their normal position (see Figure 4-4).

As a small boy growing up in northern New Jersey, we had several large Rhododendrons growing outside our dining room window. On cold winter mornings, I would look out at the plants to gauge how to dress for school that day. With experience, I found these Rhododendrons as adequate as any thermometer. In some ways, the Rhododendrons were an even better gauge, because their response was apparently due to the chill factor rather than temperature alone.

It would appear this phenomenon is not the sole prerogative of Rhododendrons. The leaves of certain Camellia hybrids also express this characteristic. This became evident to me for the first time during a prolonged cold spell we had in December 1989. The phenomenon is not as extreme among these Camellia hybrids as in Rhododendrons, but still it is apparent.

Between December 16 and 25, the maximum temperature did not go above freezing, while the minimums fluctuated between 12° and –8°F. Several of my *C. oleifera* x *C. japonica* hybrids were looking strange. Their leaves were hanging limp and tightly curled upon themselves (see Figure 4-5). I was sure I was going to have severe losses among these. Observations during the next several days showed no improvement. On December 26, after a low of 6° F early in the morning, the temperature rose to 42°F, and we had a light rain. When I went out to look at these plants again, they looked fine. Their leaves were a glossy green and had uncurled to their normal positions (Figure 4-6). It struck me that what I had witnessed was basically the same phenomena that occurred regularly on Rhododendrons nearby. During the following weeks, and on occasion in subsequent years, I have made comparable observations between the camellia hybrids and the Rhododendrons, and their response to temperature fluctuations. Interestingly, the Rhododendrons and camellia hybrids were in perfect cadence with each other.

The curling process, as expressed in both Rhododendron and

Figure 4-3 - Rhododendron leaves in response to 19°F temperatures. Cultivar 'PJM' (Weston Nurseries).

Figure 4-4 - Rhododendron 'PJM' leaves after temperatures returned to above 32° F.

Figure 4-5 - Camellia 'Spring Circus' leaves in response to 19° F temperatures.

Figure 4-6 - Camellia 'Spring Circus' leaves after temperatures returned to about 32° F.

Camellia, reduces the exposure of the lower (dorsal) leaf surface where most stomata (gas exchange pores) are located (Figure 4-7). Stomata serve as the principal pathways through which gaseous substances, such as oxygen, carbon dioxide and water vapor, enter or exit from the leaf. Protecting them from contact with dry freezing weather reduces water loss, which can be critical to plant survival.

What appeared at first to be a clear-cut plant response to environmental stress becomes confusing when one starts making comparisons among the camellias themselves. The leaf curling phenomena does not occur on either *C. oleifera* 'Lu Shan Snow' or *C. oleifera* P.I. 162561, the two main sources of cold hardiness. Also, it does not occur on any of the *C. oleifera* crosses with either *C. sasanqua* or *C. hiemalis*. Many of these have demonstrated superior cold hardiness without resorting to the leaf curling phenomena. Thus, they must depend upon other characteristics that provide them with protection against sub-zero temperatures. The *C. oleifera* x *C. japonica* hybrids fall into two classes, those whose leaves curl in response to sub-freezing temperatures and those whose leaves do not. Here, fortunately, the situation is clearer. The camellias with leaves that curl, have shown superiority to those that do not, as far as escaping injury during freezing weather. Therefore, we can assume that the leaf-curling characteristic does have a positive effect on plant survival.

E. <u>Changing Old Habits – to Break or Not to Break – the Tap Root</u>

As mentioned in Chapter III, camellias by nature are tap-rooted plants (Figure 3-1). The standard practice of breaking the taproot, although fully justifiable for growing container plants, appears to compromise the plant's survival capacity when subjected to adverse climatic conditions (cold, drought, or heat). The question arises just how much of a compromise is this? In 1984, I decided to find out.

An experiment involving two seed lots, (a) *C. japonica* Mrs. Bertha Harmes' open pollinated (O.P.), and (b) *C. oleifera* O.P. were used to test the theory. A series of frames holding 36 tapered

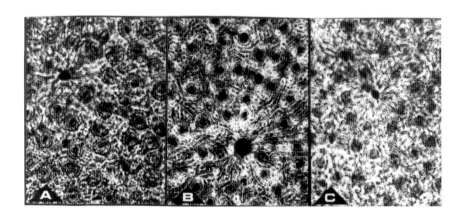

A- *C. sasanqua*   B- *C. hiemalis*   C- *C. oleifera*

Figure 4-7 - Photomicrographs of dorsal leaf surfaces of three Camellia
species showing the stomata (gas exchange pores).

tubes 4" square at the top and 14" deep, open bottomed with wire screen retainer, were used for unbroken tap root seed germination. One half of the containers were planted to seed lot (a) and one half to seed lot (b). Two seeds were planted in each container. Where both germinated, the weaker of the two was removed before it was one inch tall. Separately, standard seed flats were used for growing seedlings of the two seed lots. Here the taproots were broken at about 2" when they were transplanted from the flats to 4" pots.

Both groups of plants were grown in a greenhouse during the winter of 1985-86, and one half of each lot was planted out in late spring of 1986. At that time, the taproots of the plants in the 14" tubes were showing through the retainers at the bottom of the tubes. Planting of these was done with a post-hole digger. The other half of the seedlings, where the taproot had been broken, were planted out by the prevailing accepted methods.

Although the primary purpose of the experiment was to ascertain the value of growing tap-rooted seedlings for greater cold hardiness, the summer of 1986 provided some interesting observations. Gardeners in the Southeastern and mid-Atlantic states suffered one of the most devastating droughts in decades. Plants that were not watered regularly suffered. Even shallow rooted trees such as Dogwoods and Birch, suffered premature leaf drop. Observations of the two camellia seedling groups disclosed that those with the unbroken tap root required less watering, developed new growth sooner, were more vigorous, and did not flag or droop as did those plants whose taproot had been broken. All in all, the tap-rooted plants were more adaptable to fluctuations in climatic and soil conditions. These differences have continued through the years to the present.

Not practical from a commercial standpoint, growing seedlings in long tubes can overcome certain problems in areas presently considered too hazardous for camellias. It is quite possible for the knowledgeable gardener to grow his own seedlings this way and graft them to desired cultivars when the seedlings have attained sufficient size. I have used this system a number of times since the 1984 experiment, to successfully establish camellia plantings in particularly unfavorable locations.

F. Using Gibberellic Acid to Obtain Autumn Blooms

One of the problems of growing Spring-blooming varieties in northern climates is the potential of flower bud kill during the winter months. It is one thing to have adequate plant hardiness, but another to lose the blooms each year. There is a way to at least partially overcome this obstacle. If one treats a portion of the blooms on a spring blooming variety with gibberellic acid in late summer, then it is possible to have those flowers bloom in the Autumn. In that way, one can have both fall and spring flowers from the same plant. Also, in most cases, the flowers forced into bloom in the Fall will be larger, more attractive, and longer lasting than those produced normally in the spring.

Gibberellins are growth-regulating chemicals produced by most plants in very small quantities. The gibberellin used for camellias is gibberellic acid. The process of applying the chemical is called 'gibbing.' The application of gibberellic acid will break dormancy of the flower bud and enlarge the bloom size. The 'gib' must be applied to individual flower buds to stimulate them into action.

Gibberellic acid is available from the American Camellia Society (see References), usually in powder form, including instructions for mixing it in the proper strength (ca. 15,000 ppm) solution. If refrigerated, the solution will keep for up to a year. The powder form must be kept dry or it will deteriorate.

Gibbing a flower is a simple process. Best results come in using healthy plants, free of moisture stress, that have produced a series of large easily distinguished flower buds. Disbud if there are multiple flower buds at a single node. Break out a growth bud adjacent to a flower bud selected for treatment. This is best done with a twisting motion and should leave a small cup-like remnant at the base of the removed growth bud. Apply a drop of gibberellic acid with an eyedropper into the wound cup (Figure 4-8). One application of the solution is ample.

In Maryland, the process is normally begun in mid-August and may be extended though the end of September. The timing will differ somewhat under other climatic conditions. There is considerable variation in the blooming response time for different cultivars. In general, it ranges between 6 weeks and 3 months. Under the cool temperatures experienced in the North, response time may be more variable. If the gibbing is done over several weeks or more, on an individual cultivar, one may expect a succession of blooms.

Growers differ on the proportion of the total buds that they 'gib' on any one plant. Much of this depends on the size of the plant and how heavy a bud set. One must remember that for every treatment made, a vegetative (growth) bud next to a flower bud is sacrificed. A general rule is that a plant must be several years old and able to withstand the loss of one or more growth buds. Also, gibbing of no more than 15% of the total buds on a mature plant, produces the finest blooms and maintains the best health and vigor of the plant.

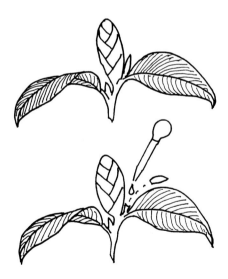

Figure 4-8 - Gibbing a growth bud next to a flower bud.

CHAPTER V

ANIMAL PROBLEMS, DISEASES, AND INSECTS

Most damage to camellias from animals, whether deer, rabbits, mice, voles, or chipmunks, occurs during the winter months when their usual source of food is scarce.

Deer

A significant problem in establishing new camellia collections at public institutions or private gardens, can be the winter feeding of deer. This is especially true in suburban areas, such as that of Washington, DC, where development sprawl has been confining local deer into smaller and smaller habitat areas. Deer normally are browsers, nibbling a few leaves here and there as they move along their daily routes. Under these circumstances, they do not cause major damage to well established larger plants. However, under severely crowded suburban conditions, even a small herd of hungry deer can completely strip a planting of several dozen tender young camellias in a single evening. Friends and correspondents living in more rural areas find deer feeding of minor significance.

If only a small number of young plants need to be protected from deer, this can be accomplished by using netting to cover individual plants, or fencing the planting. Most garden centers carry black plastic netting, which is most often used to protect fruit trees from birds. It is effective in protecting Camellia plants, and yet hardly visible from a distance.

Netting individual plants is not practical where large numbers are involved. Fencing may be necessary. The fence should be at least six feet high. However, where there is running space, closer to eight feet should be considered.

Rabbits

Rabbits are likely to be bark chewers, and, as such, can do considerable damage. Girdling of the bark of young plants just above ground level can kill them. Older plants, where the bark has become tough and rough surfaced, are not particularly vulnerable. Damage occurs most often after a snowfall, which can bury the rabbit's normal food. The easiest precaution is to place a wire cage around young plants until they are old enough to no longer be attractive.

Mice, Voles, Shrews, and other Rodents

These small mammals can do serious damage to the bark and roots of camellias and other shrubs. Voles, often incorrectly thought to be field mice, are the most common and prolific of the rodents. A single female has been known to have as many as 17 litters each year, ranging from 3-10 young. The young can start breeding when less than a month old. They are particularly widespread in the eastern and northern U.S. Meadow and pine mice are somewhat less prolific, but, nonetheless, they can also cause serious problems. They usually construct a maze of narrow runways, by means of which they feed on grass, grain, and any plant material, such as roots and bark, that are available to satisfy their voracious appetites

As with deer and rabbits, small rodent problems usually start with the onset of winter when their normal food sources are curtailed. They feed on the tender bark and roots of camellias. Often, they will make a winter nest in the mulch, at or near the base of the shrub. They burrow under the mulch to tunnel their way to other food sources. Meadow mice make runs near the surface, while pine mice runs are somewhat deeper. Both frequently use mole runways where available. One precaution is to wait until after several hard frosts before placing mulch around the base of your plants and not to put it closer than 3" from the trunk. This also prevents rotting of the bark during excessive snow cover. Hopefully, the rodents will establish their nests and feeding areas elsewhere. Also, if there is activity near the base of the camellia, it is more obvious when not hidden by a heavy mulch. A serious problem with rodent damage is that the gardener can be unaware of what is happening until spring, when the plant dies and it is discovered that much of the root system has been destroyed, or the trunk girdled.

Control consists of poison bait placed in the runways and/or at the base of the plants. Burying a ring of hardware cloth six inches deep and extending at least three inches above ground surface can be time consuming and troublesome, but is very effective. A third alternative is trapping with common mousetraps using peanut butter or apple pieces. This may be used for voles as well as mice.

Diseases and Insects

One of the distinct advantages of growing camellias outdoors north of the Camellia Belt, is the relative freedom from several serious diseases that infect camellias grown in the South. To a lesser degree, the same can be said of camellia insect problems. Whereas, **petal blight, dieback, canker,** and **tea scale**, can take a heavy toll throughout the South, the primary concern of camellia growers in the North is proper selection of the most cold-hardy-cultivars, site selection, and winter protection.

In the following pages, a brief review is made of the more troublesome diseases and insects that may affect camellias in both regions, and a comparison of the general significant of each. No effort has been made for an extensive discussion of these subjects. If a problem does arise, there is extensive information on control methods available elsewhere.

Diseases

Flower Blight is a result of the fungus '*Sclerotina camelliae*'. Considered the most devastating of camellia diseases, it has been a plague to gardeners as far north as Norfolk, VA. Where prevalent, it infects mostly spring flowering varieties of *C. japonica* and *C. reticulata,* while fall blooming *C.sasanqua* rarely becomes infected. This difference apparently is not so much because of any resistance of the latter, but because the fall blooming season does not coincide with the pathogen's infectious cycle.

In the Washington, DC, metropolitan area, petal blight appears to be confined to greenhouse-grown plants. In over forty years of observation, the author and his associates have never witnessed infected plants growing in the landscape. On the other hand, container plants purchased from southern or western nurseries, on occasion, have created epidemics in our greenhouses. Here, the infectious agent, the stone cells or sclerotia, can lie dormant in the soil of the container, only to become active late the next winter or early spring and produce a stalk on top of which is borne a small cup-shaped apothecia. From this, large numbers of spores are ejected. Spores landing on flowers cause the disease, a browning of the petals (Figure 5-1). Since there have been countless opportunities for the disease to get established outdoors in our area, it appears that our climate is not suitable for the organism to complete its life cycle.

Dieback (Also called canker and twig blight) is caused by the fungus '*Glomerella cinqulata*, and is not common in the northern regions. However, like Petal Blight, it can occur in our greenhouses. (Figure 5-2). It is a serious disease in the Southeast, and along the Gulf Coast, where temperatures and humidity remain high throughout much of the year. The disease attacks *C. sasanqua*, *C. oleifera*, and their hybrids, more severely than *C. japonica*. However, it can cause damage and plant death among all of the camellia species. This is mentioned here only because of its potential as a problem in heated greenhouses, where high humidity levels are maintained.

Armillarea Root Rot, more common in the Camellia Belt than in the North, is caused by infection from the oak-root fungus *'Armillarea mellea'*. It can be serious in areas where woodland has been reclaimed for garden use. The fungus can attack a broad spectrum of trees and shrubs, including camellias, where it can live on both dead and living tissues. Having established itself on the decaying roots left from trees removed, it can then transfer to living plants in the area. Symptoms consist of wilting and defoliation with eventual death of the plant.

Phytophthora Root Rot is caused by the water mold fungus *Phytophthora cinnamoni*. This is another broad ranging, soil-borne, fungus that appears mostly during hot weather and associated with wet, compact soils. Symptoms may appear as yellowing of foliage, smaller, limp leaves, tip dieback, and flower bud drop. In advanced cases, wilting will lead to extensive dieback and death of the plant. The fungus is spread from one area to another by the movement of soil, water, or plants, as the fungus survives in the soil and debris on the soil. Many soils are naturally infested with this fungus since it has a wide host range. This disease can be serious in soils where drainage is poor. Container-grown plants are very susceptible to this disease. In containers, a well-drained, properly aerated mix should be used. Do NOT reuse mixes or pots that have been infested with the disease-causing agent. *C. sasanqua* and *C. oleifera* are resistant to the fungus and should be used as rootstock for grafting of *C. japonica* cultivars. It is not a common problem for camellias grown in cooler regions, especially those in well-aerated soils with good drainage.

Scab is a physiological condition associated with excess moisture or fluctuations of moisture from too high to too low. There is no biological agent associated with this condition and chemical sprays are ineffective. It is believed that improvement of drainage and growing conditions are the best possible controls. Symptoms of scab are rather varied. It usually appears first as a tiny, water-soaked, and often raised area on the underside of the leaf. These spots enlarge and may become corky, brown in color, and of irregular size and shape. They do not seem to affect the health of the plant.

Sooty Mold is a surface feeder living on the sweet sticky excretions on the leaves, caused by sap-sucking insects such as aphids and various scale insects. The fungus does not penetrate the leaf tissue, but the black patches can reduce photosynthesis. Actually, its presence is an indicator of a more serious problem with some sap-sucking insect. Control the insect and wash the leaves with a mild detergent soap solution. This normally eliminates the sooty mold (Figure 5-3).

Camellia Leaf Gall, caused by the fungus *Exobasidium*, can be very disconcerting to the gardener when it is observed for the first time. It occurs mostly on *C. sasanqua, C. oleifera*, and related hybrids. The galls (Figure 5-4) consist of a gross thickening and distortion of leaves sporadically scattered over the plant and only in the spring on the new leaves. This fungus never attacks older parts of the plant. The galls can be white, pink, or gray in color, and only develop in years when environmental conditions are just right for its development. It is not a serious problem, for it rarely affects plant health. One merely removes the galls and destroys them. The fungus will not spread to other plants in the garden, and if ignored, will generally dry up in a matter of a few weeks. It is rare that it will occur again before several years time.

Insects

Scale Insects – There are a number of scale insects that affect camellias. Scales feeding on leaves, considered important in the South, such as **Tea Scale** (Figure 5-5) and **Florida Wax Scale**, are of much less significant in northern areas.

Peony Scale (Figure 5-6) feed on the trunks and branches creating sunken white spots. The young 'crawlers' secure themselves in fine cracks. A layer of bark usually grows over them protecting them from predators and weather. This also makes them less vulnerable to winter conditions in northern areas. It can be a serious problem, and if not controlled, can result in the death of badly infected plants.

As with all scale insects, the most effective controls are made during the 'crawler' stage. Fortunately, there is normally only one annual generation in northern areas compared to several in the South.

Figure 5-1 - Camellia flowers with advanced stage of Petal Blight.

Figure 5-2 - Typical Bark Canker symptoms.

Figure 5-3 - Sooty Mold, an indicator of some type of sap-sucking insect.

Figure 5-4 - Leaf Gall, sporadically infects young succulent foliage.

Aphids are mostly a problem of greenhouse plants and then primarily associated with the young growth. The easiest control is a strong spray of water directed at both upper and lower leaf surfaces.

Red Spider Mites are rarely a problem of outdoor plants in northern regions. They thrive under hot weather conditions. Leaves attacked by spider mites take on a fine reddish-brown speckled appearance much like a dusting of pepper, especially on the underside of the leaves. The upper surface of the leaves becomes a dull, silvery green. Always examine newly purchased plants for these symptoms, especially plants shipped in from the South or West Coast. Mites are most prevalent during a hot dry summer. Mites may be controlled with forceful sprays of water on both sides of the leaves at 5-7 day intervals.

Summary

Of the diseases described in this chapter, the only disease the author has experienced on landscape camellias is Leaf Gall. Its occurrence has been sporadic, happening once every 5 or 6 years, when the weather conditions (wet and hot) occur in the spring.

Likewise, insects have been limited to an occasional plant with a few oyster scales (1/4" white, raised, oyster-like bumps on the trunk). These are easily scraped off with the thumbnail. This is another reason to carefully examine newly imported plants. Where scale insects do become a problem, the systemic Cygon has proven very effective. The best method of application is to use a small brush to paint a 1" band around the trunk several inches above the soil line. One should wear plastic gloves and avoid skin contact with this toxic chemical. Opposed to the wanton use of chemicals, I have never found it necessary to use insecticides or fungicides on my garden camellias, and use them very sparingly in my greenhouse.

Should the Northern gardener feel the need to resort to using pesticides, we suggest he visit his local garden center or County Extension Agent, for information on what is suitable for his area.

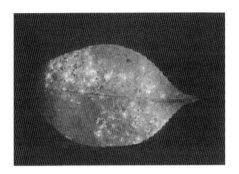

Figure 5-5 - Tea Scale, showing attack on the upper surface of the leaves

Figure 5-6 - Peony Scale, can be a very serious problem

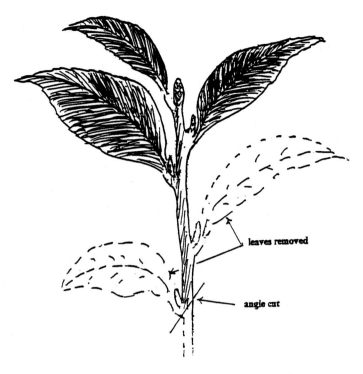

leaves removed

angle cut

Figure 6-1 A five-leaf-node cutting

wedge

Figure 6-2 Single-leaf-node cutting

CHAPTER VI

The most widely used method of propagating camellias is through the rooting of cuttings. The easiest and most flexible of the various techniques, it is adaptable to the home gardener interested in a few new plants, or to the nurseryman producing tens of thousands each year. It is also the most reliable way to obtain an exact replication of existing cultivars. There is an exception. The exact replica is of the particular twig used for a cutting. If by chance, that part of the original plant has mutated (formed a sport) to a new type of flower, that is what you will get.

Cuttings should be taken from the current season's growth. When the twig is reasonably mature, the stem color changes from green to light tan or brown, and is firm, not rubbery.

In Maryland, this occurs around mid July at the earliest and extends through to early autumn as the wood continues to harden. Some propagators prefer to wait until October or November. At this time some callusing takes place in the cutting bed, but substantial rooting is delayed until the following spring. However, the final rooted plant is claimed to be sturdier and actually catches up with those cuttings set earlier in the season.

The ideal cutting is about five leaf nodes long (Figure 6-1), but may be shorter when current growth is limited. Plants may actually be propagated from a single leaf node with a wedge of stem tissue attached (Figure 6-2). With the larger cuttings, a slanting cut is made through the base node and the lower two leaves removed, leaving three leaves intact. Wounding opposite sides of the base increases exposure of the cambium layer (green layer under the bark) and hastens rooting. The three remaining leaves, if very large (primarily among spring flowering species) may be trimmed back to a third of their length. This helps reduce crowding, and the cuttings will be less subject to dehydration.

The primary objective of the rooting media is to provide support for the cutting while allowing oxygen to reach the base of the cutting. There is no need, nor is it desirable, for the medium to supply nutrients at this stage of cutting development. Thus, the less compact and fine grained the medium, the better – potting soil should definitely be avoided. A frequently-used mixture is 75% sand and 25% peat. Unless the sand is coarse and thoroughly washed, free of any clay or silt, it should not be used. Far safer would be the use of a coarse grade of agricultural Perlite. Vermiculite is sometimes used, but it tends to break down and become denser with time. Finally, obtain a coarse grade of peat, not the ultra-fine grade found on many garden shop shelves.

Special hormones can be very useful in speeding up the rooting process. These consist of various concentrations and combinations of such compounds as IBA (Indolbutericacid), IAA (Indoaceticacid), Naphthaleneacetamide, and thiram, Trade name products widely available include Hormodin #1, #2, & #3, each stronger than its predecessor, and Rootone. The most universally used of these for Camellias is Hormodin #2, for cuttings taken mid-to-late summer; and Hormodin #3, for those taken in the fall. The hormone is applied by moistening the base of the cutting and dipping it in the rooting compound. Many nurserymen use liquid formulations of their own hormone combination which they consider superior.

The basic function of the enclosure for holding the cuttings during the rooting process is to provide conditions of high humidity, designed to prevent the cuttings from drying out. This may consist of a flowerpot filled with the proper medium to hold the cuttings, covered with an inverted glass jar, or plastic bag, supported by several plant labels. This is an easy system for the small gardener.

Enclosures may be expanded to flats, or other receptacles, covered with an appropriately-sized plastic covered frame. A more complex arrangement consists of special raised greenhouse benches equipped with electric heating cables below the rooting medium to provide heat to the base of the cuttings. To prevent dehydration in this 'open system', automatic overhead intermittent mist is provided, controlled by either an electronic leaf or a time clock.

The advantage of the intermittent 'open' mist system over the inverted jar or other enclosed system, is that it operates most efficiently in full sun, whereas any 'enclosed' system would greatly overheat unless in filtered shade.

Under normal conditions, cuttings taken in mid-summer should root in about six to eight weeks. This, however, can vary with the prevailing conditions. Fall cuttings should be well rooted by the next spring.

Grafting

There are several reasons why camellias may be grafted instead of being propagated by cuttings or other vegetative methods. Most important of these is the ability to convert an unwanted seedling or cultivar, into a plant with flowers more to the grower's liking. Successfully grafted plants grow rapidly and come into flower sooner than with most other methods of propagation.

The large root system in relation to the top, stimulates very rapid growth and early flowering. Plant breeders interested in seeing flowers from their hybrid crosses as soon as possible take advantage of this phenomenon. A scion taken from a small hybrid seedling and grafted onto a healthy rootstock, will flower years before the seedling itself would flower. In addition, some camellias do not root readily from cuttings, especially cuttings of *C. reticulata*.

Successful grafts are dependent upon good vigorously growing rootstocks and sound healthy scions. Weak spindly growth of either is a prelude to failure. Both *C. japonica* and *C. sasanqua* rootstocks are commonly used and personal preferences vary as to their virtues. For the beginner, a stock with a ½" to ¾" trunk diameter is the most suitable.. Larger or smaller diameters, although perfectly satisfactory, do require some degree of prior experience for success.

The primary function in grafting is to unite the cambium tissue of the scion (green layer) , with that of the rootstock, and not have the scion dry out during the process. The most optimum time to graft in the Northeast is from January through March. However, it may extend to almost any month except during the spring and early summer while active growth is in progress. By collecting the desired scions early, before growth begins, and storing them slightly moistened in sealed plastic bags in the refrigerator (45°F), even spring grafting is possible.

The problem of preventing the scions from drying out can be overcome in a number of ways. The easiest procedure is to invert a wide-mouthed glass jar, large enough to enclose the cut-off stock with scion in place. An alternate method is to attach two sticks to the base of the stock that will protrude above the scion, and then covering both sticks and scion with an inverted plastic bag tied snugly around the stock below the graft union. The sticks provide support for the plastic bag, and prevent it from bearing down on the scion. To avoid possible overheating, keep covered grafted plants away from direct sun. A north-facing window should provide both adequate light and protection. Where this is not practical, burlap sun shields can serve a useful purpose.

The tools required include:

A very sharp knife or single-edged razor blade
A pruning shears, and/or a fine-toothed saw
Rubber bands
Screwdriver
Soft twine
Large-mouthed glass jars, or plastic bags, or gallon plastic milk jugs, whose bottoms have been cut off.
Some sturdy small diameter sticks.

Beyond these basic implements, there are other materials considered essential by some grafters. These include:

Fungicides placed on exposed cut surfaces
Rooting hormone
Aluminum foil to cover the scion/stock union

All of these are in an effort to help promote callus formation, the precursor of a good union.

Grafting Methods

Cleft Grafts

Among the various Camellia grafting techniques, the cleft graft is probably the most widely used. The process is begun with the cutting off of the trunk of the rootstock, (at least pencil diameter or larger), with shears or saw, about four inches above the soil level and then smoothing any rough edges with a knife. A vertical cut is made down through the middle of the top, extending about two inches down the sides. On stocks one-inch in diameter, or less, the more suitable of the two sides is chosen and a slanting cut is made up from the opposite side to the middle of the stock (Figure 6-3a). This helps the eventual callusing over of the wound. A screwdriver is forced down through the middle of the crack, spreading it, to make room for the scion (Figure 6-3b).

The scion ideally consists of about five leaves with the lower two removed. A beveled cut about an inch long is made down opposite sides to the base (Figure 6-3c), to form a wedge with one side slightly wider than the other. The scion is slipped down into the cut along the good side with the wider portion of the wedge to the outside (Figure 6-3d). The trick here is to line up the cambium (green) layer of the scion with that of the stock, or at least make it cross over the other by slanting the scion slightly outward. A small portion, 1/8 inch, of the cut surface should extend above the stock so that callus will form over the tip. The screwdriver is then gently removed, which should make the slit in the stock close snugly against the scion. This will be made even more closely fitting by wrapping a rubber band tightly around the stock (Figure 6-3e). Success of the graft will depend upon the union of the two cambium (green tissue) layers, creating a continuous bond between stock and scion. The graft is then ready for its protective covering to prevent drying (Figure 6-3f). If the stock is larger in diameter than one inch, two scions on opposite sides of the split stock may be inserted instead of one. The only difference here is that the slanted cut of the stock is not necessary.

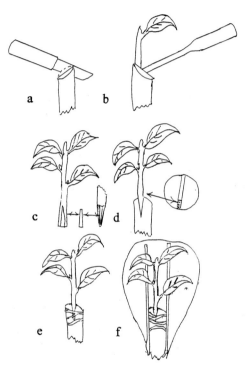

Figure 6-3 Steps in compleing a cleft graft

a. Cut-off stock is split with a sharp knife.
b. A screwdriver forces the split apart to make room for the scion.
c. Prepared scion with beveled cuts down opposite sides to the base.
d. Scion in its proper position on stock with the matching of the cambium (green) layers of the scion with the stock.
e. Completed graft, wrapped with rubber band.
f. Completed graft covered with a plastic bag supported by wooden sticks.

Bark Grafts

Mostly used in late spring or early summer to accommodate dormant scions received from a colder region, or scions collected earlier and held in a refrigerator. At this time, the bark is slipping and the rootstock has begun its flush of spring growth. The rootstock is cut off in a similar manner as that done for a cleft graft. However, instead of cutting down through the middle of the stock, a cut is made about 1-1/2 inches down one side, through the bark to the woody tissue. The bark is then loosened on each side of the cut from top to bottom. The scion is cut beveled on one side with a slanting cut about 1-3/4 inches long (Figure 6-4). With the beveled side against the woody tissue, the scion is slid down through the center of the vertical cut in the stock. As with the cleft graft, leave about 1/8" cut surface exposed above the rootstock. Some grafters drive a fine nail through the middle of the slanted cut into the woody tissue to help secure the scion. This is followed by securely wrapping the scion against the stock with rubber bands or other materials. The grafted scion is then ready for covering.

Whip Grafts

This form of grafting is usually reserved for rootstocks that have trunk diameters approximately pencil size. The best results come when the scion and rootstock have the same diameter. If the scion is smaller, then the cambium on one side should be matched on that side only. Robust scions of good substance are best for this procedure. A sloping cut 1-1/2 inches long is made on the scion to exactly match a comparable sloping cut on the rootstock. Both cuts are notched, forming a tongue on each (Figure 6-5) positioned so that when locked together, the cambium (green tissue) of the scion fully matches that of the stock, in several places. The graft union is wrapped tightly with a rubber band. The grafted scion is then ready for covering similar to the other grafting techniques described.

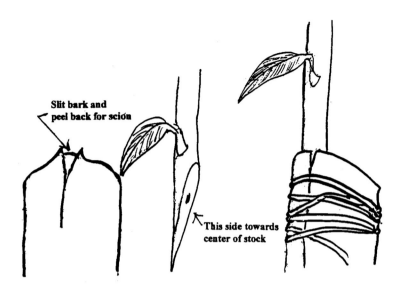

Figure 6-4 Bark Graft

Figure 6-5 Whip Graft

Hardening Off

Grafts normally knit in about six weeks. Then, the first steps may be taken in hardening off. The formation of callus tissue around the points of scion/stock contact on either cleft or bark grafts is a good indication that a successful union has been made.

However, it is still best not to be premature in completely removing the cover. Also, since the scion has spent six weeks at relatively high humidity within its enclosure, it may be a shock if suddenly exposed to the outside air.

If the graft is covered with an inverted jar, raising the jar an inch or so and placing several small blocks underneath should be adequate. If covered by a gallon milk jug, the first step is to remove the screw top cover. If covered with a disposable plastic bag, a number of slits in the upper portion of the bag are in order. In all cases, the amount of exposure should be gradually increased over the following several weeks. If any graft scion wilts, replace the covering for another week.

Since whip graft unions are completely covered, inspection for callus development is impractical. Removing the bindings at this stage can be hazardous. The cautious grafter waits until there are definite signs of growth in the scion before proceeding in the hardening off process. One caution for any grafted plant, is the tendency to give it too much water. Remember, you have removed the top of the rootstock and replaced it with a covered scion. Thus, there will be no moisture loss except from the container and its medium. Some experienced grafters do no watering at all from the time of initial grafting until the scion graft is completely uncovered.

Air Layers

A distinct advantage of this method of propagation is that relatively large plants can be produced in one season's time. Also, for the inexperienced grower, a much higher degree of success may be anticipated here compared to using any of the grafting methods. Performed in the spring, after the last killing frost, the treated branches can be left on their own throughout the summer, during which time the rooting takes place. The air layers are then harvested in late autumn before the danger of hard freezes. One possible drawback is that rather large donor plants with good, vigorous growth are necessary from which branches can be sacrificed.

The materials needed include:

A sharp knife or single blade razor
A container of moistened shredded sphagnum moss
Aluminum foil cut into 8 x 8 inch squares (to protect from bird damage)
A number of pieces of plastic film (4 mil thick preferred) cut into 8 x 8 inch squares
Rooting hormone
Plant twisties, rubber bands, or soft twine

Air layering is a modification of the ancient Chinese technique of ground layering, in which a branch is bent down to ground level, wounded and covered with soil.

Most camellia branches are not amenable to being bent to ground level. Air layering simply involves artificially bringing a soil substitute up to the branch level.

The rooting process involves breaking the flow of sap through the phloem (bark) from the branch leaves down to the main branches and roots. This is done by removing a ring of bark an inch wide and scraping all the cambium (green) off in that area.. Nutrients produced in the leaves through photosynthesis tend to accumulate at the scraped ring site and stimulate the formation of roots.

After the ring of bark has been removed and scraped clean of all signs of cambium tissue, it is dusted with rooting hormone. A fistful of moist sphagnum (about the size of a large grapefruit) is squeezed free of excessive water, divided down the middle and molded around the treated area (Figure 6-6). This is then wrapped with a square of aluminum foil (Figure 6-7), tightly squeezed at each end and then covered with a square of plastic overlapped about 2 inches to protect the foil from bird pecks, branch tears, etc. The next step takes a bit of dexterity, or two people working together. Holding the plastic firmly in place, the opposite ends need to be gathered snugly around the branch and tied shut, making a moisture-sealed unit (Figure 6-8).

Properly moisture-sealed air layers should not require attention during the summer. However, it is well to periodically examine a few for drying out of the sphagnum. This is also the time to look for the appearance of roots poking through the sphagnum to the inner side of the covering. Drying out can be remedied by adding water through a syringe, or by removing the top twistie, plastic, and foil, and moistening, before resealing.

The harvesting of air layers in the fall is accomplished by cutting off the branch on the trunk side of the air layer, several inches below the wrapping. After removing the plastic covering and the foil, as much of the sphagnum moss as is possible, should be CAREFULLY removed without injury to the roots (Figure 6-9). The air-layered plant is then ready for potting up in a loose medium, such as composted pine bark. Frequently, these plants have restricted root systems in relation to their tops and need close attention to watering and should be kept in a shaded location until they become fully established. Wire hoops or stakes may be necessary to provide stability to the new plant until it has established a firm root foundation.

Seed Germination

While asexual propagation (rooted cuttings, grafts, air layers, etc) will produce individuals identical to the parent from which the propagation materials are taken, seed propagation produces progeny genetically different. Since Camellias (unlike most garden vegetables) are highly heterozygous, the offspring are individuals unto themselves, and may only resemble the parent superficially, even from self-pollinations. Also, very few seedlings approach the flower quality and performance of the parents. Yet, it is through

Figure 6-6 - Air layer with a ball of moist sphagnum.

Figure 6-7 - Wrapping air layer with square of aluminum foil.

Figure 6-8 - The aluminum foil wrap covered by a plastic wrap to help reduce bird punctures.

Figure 6-9 - Air layer harvested in the fall, showing mass of roots which developed.

hybridization and seed production that new and better varieties are developed. The topic of breeding and techniques of making controlled crosses will be discussed in detail in Chapter VII.

Camellia seeds normally mature from early September through late October. Most fall blooming camellias, such as *C. sasanqua* and *C. oleifera,* produce capsules containing one to three seeds, while spring blooming *C. japonica* may contain as many as eight. Most capsules are bright green, rather leathery in consistency, and range in size from ¾" to 2" in diameter. Those exposed to full sun frequently take on a deep maroon red blush and somewhat resemble small apples. When mature, the outer coat splits into several segments, spilling the seeds onto the ground. The loss of seeds may be prevented by fastening nylon net bags (never use plastic) around the capsules.

The seeds themselves have an outer coat that is black, hard, and impervious to water. Germination may be hastened by carefully scarifying this hard coat with a file or knife blade. It is important to expose the parchment-like inner coat without digging into the seed itself, which can lead to fungus infection.

Plants native to regions where the winter temperatures go well below freezing, produce seeds that require a period of chilling before they will germinate. If they did not have this built-in dormancy and the seeds germinated and grew into tender seedlings in early autumn, they would not survive the winter. In nature, such plants would not produce replacement generations and would soon die out.

The range of camellias in the Orient extends from Sub-Tropical to cool Temperate Zones. Thus, it might be expected that the seed dormancy requirements differ from the southern to northern regions. Since the camellias involved in this book fall mostly in the latter category, for good germination, it should be assumed that the seeds will require a chilling period of at least 5 weeks.

Camellia books written by southern authors rarely mention the need for a moist cold treatment (stratification) to obtain germination and vigorous seedling growth. This may be appropriate for the seeds of the particular camellia cultivars they are handling. However, if followed by growers working with seeds of the more cold hardy cultivars, it can lead to greatly reduced germination and poor growth of those that eventually do germinate. Also, there appears to be a strong tendency for the development of roots, but no shoots, among seedlings where there has been insufficient chilling exposure.

There are two basic methods for providing the necessary chilling experience; let nature do it, or do it artificially. In the first method, the seeds are planted out in early autumn, in a well worked, well-drained garden soil. The seeds should be planted no deeper than the seed diameter. The biggest problem is their possible destruction during the winter by mice or squirrels. A sheet of ½" hardware cloth will help protect them.

The second method is to soak the seeds in a 1:10 solution of household bleach overnight. Then, mix them thoroughly in sterilized sphagnum peat or other moisture retaining medium, which is first soaked and then squeezed to remove excess water. Seed and sphagnum are put in plastic bags, sealed, and dated prior to their placement in a refrigerator for 5 to 6 weeks at about 40°F

After the cold treatment period, the seed is removed from the sphagnum and is ready to be planted. Small quantities may be planted in pots that can then be set on top of a hot water heater. This will provide bottom heat, which speeds up germination. Larger quantities of seed are best planted in flats and placed in a heated greenhouse, sun porch, or other facility suitable for germination. A glass or plastic covering over the container, is helpful in preventing drying out.

Camellias are basically tap-rooted plants (as described in Chapter IV). Whether to break the taproot, or not, will depend largely on the ultimate use of the seedling. This will differ as to whether it is to be grown in a container or in the ground. For the container, breaking the taproot will create the desired spreading root system. On the other hand, tap-rooted seedlings would be more adaptable to prevailing severe weather conditions beyond the Camellia belt by allowing for deeper rooting in the ground.

CHAPTER VII

BREEDING NEW CAMELLIAS

Hybridizing Can Be Fun

Creating a new camellia can provide the pleasure of anticipation, followed by the realization of having developed something original. You do not have to be a professional breeder. Many outstanding camellia cultivars have been developed by backyard hobbyists. Expensive equipment is not required. All that is needed are a few well-selected plants as prospective parents. This can be expanded in complexity to suit the interests of the gardener.

For those wishing to go beyond the standard cultivars as parents, some lesser-known species are readily available. Perhaps the most comprehensive source is *Nuccio's Nurseries*, 3555 Chaney Trail, Altadena, CA 91001. Phone: 626-794-3383. They list some 35 minor species in their catalog. Detailed descriptions of these, and many other species, are given in the back of *The Camellia Nomenclature,* A. Gonos and S. Bracci, Editors. (see References).

Progress Through the Years

Most early camellia cultivars were the result of selections made among open-pollinated seedlings where records may or may not have been kept of the seed parent, and any attempt at identifying the pollen parent was highly speculative. However, the twentieth century has seen extensive use of controlled crosses, within spring-flowering *Camellia japonica and C. reticulata* and fall-flowering *C. sasanqua* and *C. hiemalis*. The vast number of registered cultivars now in existence is strong evidence that camellia growers have been busy.

During the past 60 years systematic hybridization procedures involving detailed records have been followed. Technically, hybridization may occur at three stages, each progressively more difficult to accomplish. These levels are **intraspecific, interspecific,** and **intergeneric** hybridization. An **intraspecific** cross may, for example, occur between two *Camellia japonica* individuals and will yield a *C. japonica* seedling. An **interspecific** cross combines members of two, or more species, into one hybrid individual. An example would be *C. sasanqua* crossed with *C. oleifera*. When hybridization goes a step further and plants from two related genera are successfully crossed, then an **intergeneric** hybrid has been formed. Such hybrids are exceedingly rare, but do exist. For example, that of *Camellia japonica X alatamaha* (Ackerman and Williams 1982).

Why We Need More Interspecific Hybrids

Although most breeding work to date has been done within a very narrow group of species, more than 270 species exist within the genus *Camellia* (details in Chapter I). More new species are becoming available each year from the People's Republic of China. Here is a source for progress in the utilization of genetic diversification. Most of the minor species have small flowers of limited commercial value, and are difficult to hybridize with commercial cultivars.It takes many years of crossing and backcrossing to get hybrids that are commercially acceptable. Yet, continued breeding solely within the major horticultural species has reached the stage of diminishing returns within the restricted gene pool. Only by utilizing minor species can we acquire such traits as pleasing floral fragrance; greater tolerance to cold or heat and light intensity; yellow, blue, or purple flower color; new dwarf plant forms; and an extended blooming season.

Important Traits and Breeding Objectives

Significant progress comes where there is a clear-cut objective. It is not enough to hybridize haphazardly in hopes of some unforeseen improvement. Thus, you do well to plan ahead, establish an objective, select plant specimens possessing at least one or more of the desired genetic characteristics, and then cross those, to produce the desired objective. Three goals that have had a degree of success over the past several decades are the search for floral fragrance, greater cold hardiness, and yellow flower color.

The Mechanics of Hybridization

Camellia, a monoecious genus, has bisexual flowers containing both male (stamen) and female (pistil) reproductive organs on the same flower (Figure 7-1A). The stamens consist of the anthers (producing pollen grains) borne on stalks or filaments. The pistil consists of an ovary at the base supporting the style, which is topped with the stigma (Figure 7-1B). Pollination takes place through the activities of a wide range of flying insects. Hand pollination consists of placing mature pollen, from the desired male parent, onto a receptive stigma of the desired female parent. Important precautions are necessary to prevent unwanted pollen from contaminating the cross. This process assures knowing and controlling the parentage.

Basic procedures necessary for successful pollinations are as follows:

1. Select flowers in the balloon stage - almost but not quite open (Figure 7-1C). If out-of-doors and subject to insect activity, the flower must not be open, even slightly. If crosses are being made within a screened greenhouse, these precautions are less critical.
2. Emasculate the flower. This involves removing the anthers to prevent self pollination (Figure 7-1D), and then cutting off a portion of the petals to expose the reproductive parts.

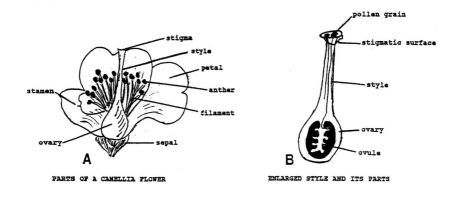

A
PARTS OF A CAMELLIA FLOWER

stigma
style
petal
stamen
anther
filament
ovary
sepal

B
ENLARGED STYLE AND ITS PARTS

pollen grain
stigmatic surface
style
ovary
ovule

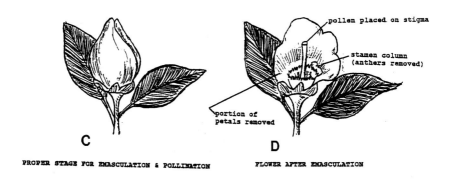

C
PROPER STAGE FOR EMASCULATION & POLLINATION

D
FLOWER AFTER EMASCULATION

pollen placed on stigma
stamen column
(anthers removed)
portion of
petals removed

Figure 7-1 Typical Camellia flowers showing reproductive organs and
proper stage for emasculation

Use a sharp knife, razor blade, or surgical scissors (Figure 7-2). Next, use tweezers, to remove the anthers and expose the pistil with its stigma (Figure 7-3)

3. Place the desired pollen on the stigma of the emasculated flower. There are several ways of doing this:

    a. Tweezers can be used to remove one or more stamens, with mature anthers, from the desired male parent, and the pollen rubbed onto the stigma of the desired female parent (Figure 7-4).

    b. A small camel's-hair brush, toothpick, wooden matchstick, or your index fingertip (Figure 7-5) may also be used to transfer pollen. The choice of instrument depends largely on whether fresh or stored pollen is used and whether the pollen is plentiful. The camel's-hair brush is the most wasteful. Whatever instrument is used, it should be sterilized with rubbing alcohol between each successive use of a different pollen.

4. Labels should be applied immediately after completing the cross. Most important is to record the date and pollen parent. If large numbers of crosses are made, the seed parent may be added later on those crosses that take. This can be labor-saving, especially with interspecific crosses where expected success rates are low. Use a pencil or indelible ink on durable labels that will withstand weather conditions for at least 8 months, and still be readable. Hang the label as close to the flower as possible, to prevent confusion with other nearby blooms.

5. Whether to cover the pollinated flower is largely dependent on the chances of contamination. Outdoor blooms are, of course, the most susceptible, but even here, a properly emasculated flower is of little attraction to insects. When flowers are to be covered, bags made of nylon netting are favored, for they allow air circulation without heat buildup. However, paper bags may be used. Never use plastic bags.

6. Aftercare. When a seed capsule matures (in from 6 to 10 months depending on the species), it splits open and expels from one to eight seeds. It is important to cover the capsule

Figure 7-2 Emasculating the flower by using a pair of surgical scissors.

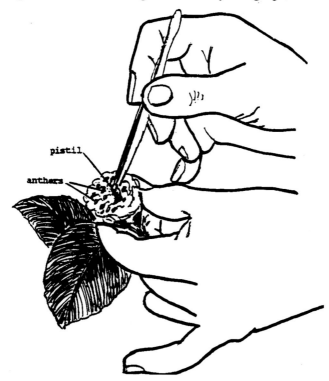

Figure 7-3 Removing anthers with tweezers to expose the pistil with its stigma.

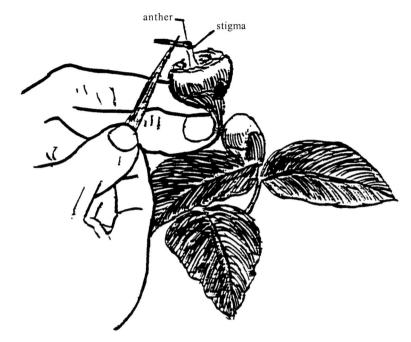

Figure 7-4 Pollination using a stamen with anther from pollen parent, and applying it to the stigma.

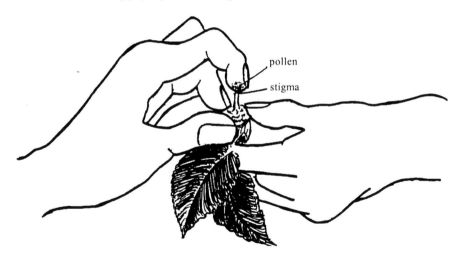

Figure 7-5 Pollination using the index finger to apply pollen to the stigma.

with a bag to catch the seed before they spill on the ground. Nylon net or old nylon stockings sewn into small bags, do quite well.

Records are extremely important. Keep a special book for recording crosses at the time they are made. Where many parents are used, a record book identifies those potential combinations that are the most productive in producing offspring. Later, separate records will be needed at the time of harvesting and planting, and finally, to identify each resulting seedling. Various coding methods may be used to indicate the individual parentage. An excellent system is to use the last two digits of the year, followed by a dash and then the successive seedling number potted up. Thus, 95-35 would be the thirty-fifth seedling potted in 1995. This information should be recorded, along with the parentage. In recording each cross, the seed parent is always placed first, followed by an "x" and then the pollen parent. For example: *Frost Princess x Snow Flurry.*

The plants to be used in achieving your objectives may not flower at the same time. Therefore, the use of fresh pollen may be impossible, or at least impractical. There are two possible solutions. One is through the use of gibberellic acid (see Chapter IV Special Situations), and the other is to collect and store pollen in advance. In the first, where a spring flowering *C. japonica* is to be crossed with fall flowering *C. oleifera,* flowers of *C. japonica* are treated with gibberellic acid in late summer. This will cause them to bloom in the Fall. Fresh pollen may then be collected and used to pollinate flowers of *C. oleifera* in its season. The second method involves gathering anthers in advance and storing them for later use. Anthers should be gathered near the time of pollen dehiscence(pollen release) and filaments should be removed. Spread the anthers out to dry on a sheet of hard-surfaced paper for several days at room temperature. The anthers are then funneled into small glass vials and plugged with cotton. The vials, in turn, are stored in a specially prepared screw-top jar. Place a 1 to 2-inch (2.5-5 cm.) layer of silica gel, or anhydrous calcium chloride in the bottom of the jar and cover with cotton. A number of glass vials of anthers can be stored in one jar. Place the jar in a refrigerator for short-term storage, or in the freezer, if storage is longer than several weeks. Remember, moisture is the pollen's worst enemy! If properly air-dried and stored, *Camellia* pollen may be held for more than 8 months and still retain substantial viability.

'Berenice Boddy'

'R.L. Wheeler'

'Mathotiana Supreme'

'Lady Clare'

'Paulette Goddard'

'Rev. John Drayton'

CHAPTER VIII

COMMERCIAL CAMELLIAS PROVEN SUITABLE FOR REGIONS NORTH OF THE CAMELLIA BELT

Commercial spring-blooming _Japonica_ cultivars field tested in the Washington-Baltimore metropolitan area over a forty-year period are recommended for Zones 6a-6b.

Individuals are rated for hardiness with the following **Hardiness Key:**:

   *** **Very Hardy**
    ** **Hardy**
     * **Marginally Hardy**

'Berenice Boddy' – Light pink with deep pink underpetals. Medium, semi-double. Vigorous, upright growth. Mid-season. ***

'Blood of China' – Deep salmon red. Medium, semidouble to loose, peony form. Vigorous, compact growth. Late. **

'C.M. Hovey' (Colonel Firey) – Dark red, medium, formal double. Average, slender, upright growth. Late. **

'C.M. Wilson' – Light pink sport of Elegans (Chandler). Variegated. Large to very large, anemone form. Early to mid-season. **

'Daikagura' – Bright rose pink, blotched white (also a pink and red form), Medium large, peony. Slow compact growth. Early. **

'Donckelarii' – Red, marbled white in varying degrees (also a red form). Large, semi-double. Slow, bushy growth. Mid-season. **

'Dr. Tinsley' – Very pale pink at base shading to deeper pink, with reverse side flesh pink. Medium, semi-double. Compact, upright growth. Mid-season. **

'Eleanor Hagood' – Pale pink, medium, formal double. Vigorous, upright growth. Late. *

'Elegans' (Chandler) – Rose pink with center petaloids often spotted white. Large to very large, anemone form. Slow, spreading growth. Early to mid-season. *

'Flame' – Deep flame red. Medium to large semi-double. Vigorous, upright, compact growth. Mid-season. *

'Glen 40' – Deep red. Medium to large, formal double to rose form double. Slow, upright, compact growth. Midseason to late. *

'Governor Mouton' – Oriental red, sometimes blotched white. Medium, semi-double to loose peony form. Vigorous, upright growth. Midseason. ***

'Herme' – Pink with irregular white border and streaked deep pink. Medium, semi-double. Vigorous, upright growth. Midseason. *

'Kumasaka' – Rose pink, medium, peony form to rose form double. Vigorous, compact growth. Midseason to late. ***

'Lady Clare' – Deep pink. Large, semi-double. Vigorous, bushy growth. Early to midseason. ***

'Lady Vansittart' – White, striped rose pink (also a number of color sports). Medium semi-double with broad, wavy-edged petals. Slow, bushy growth with dark green, glossy holly-like foliage. Midseason to late. **

'Leucantha' – White form of 'Tricolor (Siebold)'. Medium, semi-double of slightly cupped form. Vigorous, compact, upright growth. Midseason. ***

'Magnoliaeflora' – Blush pink, medium, semi-double. Average, compact growth. Midseason. *

'Mathotiana' – Crimson, sometimes with a purple cast. (also, a number of color sports). Large to very large. Rose form double to formal double, and a semi-double form. Vigorous, compact, upright growth. Midseason to late. **

'C.M. Hovey'   'Donckelarii'

'Kumasaka'   'Blood of China'

'Governor Mouton'   'Magnoliaeflora'

'**Meredith**' – Pale pink to crimson edges, Medium large, Semi-double to peony. Average, compact growth. ***

'**Monjisu**' – Cherry red marbled white. Medium, rose form double. Slow, bushy growth. Midseason…**

'**Paulette Goddard**' – Dark red. (also a variegated form). Medium, semi-double to loose peony to anemone form. Vigorous, upright growth. Midseason to late. ***

'**Pink Perfection**' – Shell pink. Small, formal double. Vigorous, upright growth. Early to late. *

'**Professor Charles Sargent**' – Deep red. (also a variegated form). Medium, full peony form. Vigorous, compact, upright growth. Midseason. **

'**R.L. Wheeler**' – Rose pink. (also a variegated form). Very large, semi-double to anemone form with heavy outer petals and solid circle of stamens. Vigorous, upright growth. Early to midseason. ***

'**Reverend John G. Drayton**' – Light pink. Medium, semi-double to loose peony form. Vigorous, compact, upright growth. Midseason to late. **

'**Tricolor**' (Siebold) – Waxy white, streaked carmine. (also a red sport, and a white form). Medium, semi-double of slightly cupped form. Vigorous, compact, upright growth. Midseason. ***

'**White Empress**' – White, large, semi-double with fluted petals. Vigorous, compact, upright growth. Early to midseason. *

Cultivars of Fall Blooming *C. sasanqua* field tested in the Washington-Baltimore metropolitan area with their hardiness degree, as above:

'**Agnes O. Solomon**' – Light pink. Loose, semi-double to peony form. ***

'**Cleopatra**' – Rose pink. (also a white, and a blush pink form). Medium, semi-double. *

'**Hana-Jiman**' – White, edged pink. Medium, semi-double. *

'**Jean May**' – Shell pink. Medium, rose form double. ***

'**Setsugekka**' – White, large, semi-double. *

'**Yuletide**' – Red, small single. *

Cultivars of *C. hiemalis* tested in the same area:

'**Kanjiro**' – Rose pink shading to rose red on edges of petals. Small to medium. semi-double. **

'**Showa-no-sakae**' — Soft pink, occasionally marbled white. Small to medium, semi-double to rose form double. *

CHAPTER IX

CAMELLIA INTRODUCTIONS BRED SPECIFICALLY FOR THEIR COLD HARDINESS POTENTIAL

A. <u>Sources of Greater Cold Hardiness</u>

C. oleifera 'Lu Shan Snow' (PI 162475) was introduced in 1948 as seed from Lu Shan Botanical Garden, Kuling, People's Republic of China. Later, a specimen plant was established in the U.S. National Arboretum's camellia collection. The plant has flourished since its original introduction and conceivably may be the largest specimen of *C. oleifera* outside the Orient. In 1994, at 46 years old, it measured 24' in height, and 30' in spread. (Figure 2-1). The bark on the trunks and main branches is a very attractive powdery cinnamon color (Figure 2-2). This is a characteristic that does not transmit well to its hybrid seedlings. In 1979, a propagation was established on the author's property, where it has been under evaluation through to the present.

Because of its outstanding characteristics as an attractive cold-hardy landscape plant, it was given cultivar status in 1995. The leaves are leathery, semi-glossy, very dark green with coarsely serrate margins. The flowers are three inches across, white, single, with five narrow petals and a bright orange-yellow central cluster of anthers. The blooming season extends from October to November, frequently over six weeks in duration. Unfortunately, the flowers shatter badly when cut and even when left on the shrub.

C. oleifera (PI 162561) was introduced as seed from the Botanic Garden, Sun Yat-Sen's Memorial Park Commission,

Nanking, Peoples Republic of China in 1948. Later, a specimen plant was established at the U.S. Plant Introduction Station, Glenn Dale, Maryland and propagations established in 1972 on the author's property at Ashton, Maryland, where it has been under evaluation through to the present.

The plant, not as ornamentally attractive as 'Lu Shan Snow', has none-the-less proven itself to be extremely cold hardy and a valuable breeding parent. *C. oleifera* (PI 162561) makes a compact, globular, to somewhat upright, shrub with dull gray bark, leathery semi-glossy, dark green leaves. Unfortunately, the original plant at the Glenn Dale Plant Introduction Station was destroyed during a renovation project before any plant size measurements could be obtained. The flowers are three inches across, white, single, seem more frost resistant than other camellia flowers, and tend to shatter, but not as badly as those of 'Lu Shan Snow'. Flower buds mature over a long period of time causing an extended blooming season from early October through to early December. Among eight *C. oleifera* introductions from Asia field tested over the years, only 'Lu Shan Snow' and PI 162561, proved reliably cold hardy. These two were long considered to be of equal hardiness. However, 'Lu Shan Snow; suffered modest leaf damage following a series of temperatures down to –15°F, while PI 162561 remained untouched.

B. **Interspecific Hybrid Cultivars-Fall-Winter Blooming**

Blooming times are those recorded during an average season in Maryland. These dates may differ under the prevailing climatic conditions in other areas. Also, considerable variability can exist when dealing with cultivars resulting from crosses between fall blooming *C. oleifera* and spring blooming *C. japonica*. Each parent's normal blooming season, determined by its genetic makeup, influences the season of its offspring, to a greater or lesser degree. Thus, such varieties as 'Ashton's Pink', Ashton's Snow, 'Fairweather Favorite', 'Winter's Beauty', and 'Winter's Moonlight', have blooming seasons extending from early to late winter rather than either fall or spring.

Listed Below are the Cold Hardy Hybrids from the Author's Breeding Program That Have Been Registered with the American Camellia Society to Date:

'Ashton's Ballet' – *C. japonica* 'Shikishima X *C. oleifera* (PI 162561). Compact, moderately upright, average growth. Makes a beautiful garden specimen. Flowers are two-tone pink, rose form double. Blooms from early November to late December. Cold hardy to – 10°F.

'Ashton's Pink' – *C. japonica* 'Billie McCaskill' X *C. oleifera* (PI 162561). Dense, upright, average growth, dark green foliage. Forms a symmetrical plant without pruning. Flowers are lavender pink, semi-double, Long blooming season from December to February. Cold hardy to –10°F.

'Ashton's Pride' — *C. oleifera* (PI 162561) X *C. sasanqua* ''Santozaki'. Vigorous, spreading, small narrow, leathery, medium-green leaves. Heavy bud setter. Flowers are pale pink, single. Blooms from mid-November to mid-December. Cold hardy to –15°F.

'Ashton's Snow' – *C. japonica* 'Billie McCaskell' X *C. oleifera* (PI 162561). Moderate, globular, dense growth. Leaves thick, leathery, semi-glossy, dark green. Flowers are white, semi-double. Long blooming season, beginning in early November and ending in late January. Cold haryd to –15°F.

'Elaine Lee' – *C. japonica* 'Mrs. Bertha Harmes' X *C. oleifera* (PI 162561). Plant is compact, average vigor, upright in growth. Leaves dark green, glossy. Flowers are white, semi-double, especially hardy. Blooms from November, sporadically, through January. Cold hardy to –10°F.

'Fairweather Favorite' – *C. japonica* 'Frost Queen' X *C. oleifera* (PI 162561). Dense, upright, medium growth. Leaves leathery, glossy, dark green. Makes a very compact handsome specimen. Very floriferous. Flowers, white with pink underside, semi-double. Long blooming season from late-November through January. Cold hardy to –15°F.

'Frost Prince' – *C. hiemalis* 'Shishi-gashira X *C. oleifera* (PI 162561). Moderately vigorous, globular growth. Very floriferous. Flowers are deep pink single to semi-double to anemone form. Blooms from mid October to November. Cold hardy to –5°F.

'Ashton's Pride'

'Winter's Rose'

'Ashton's Pride'

'Winter's Rose'

'Polar Ice'   'Winter's Dream'

'Winter's Charm'   'Winter's Star'

'Frost Princess' – *C. hiemalis* 'Bill Wylam' X *C. oleifera* (PI 162561). Compact, globular growth. Flowers are deep iridescent lavender pink, semi-double to anemone form. Blooms from early November to mid-December. Cold hardy to –5°F.

'Polar Ice' — 'Frost Princess' X *C. oleifera* (PI 162561). Slow to moderate growth with arching branches. Flowers are white, anemone form. Blooms from early November to mid-December. Cold hardy to –10°F.

'Snow Flurry' — *C. oleifera* (PI 162561) X 'Frost Princess'. Moderately vigorous, globular to spreading, with arching branches. Very floriferous, blooming at an early age. Flowers are white, full peony to anemone form. The earliest of the fall blooming series, it flowers from late September to mid-November. Cold hardy to –10°F..

'Winter's Beauty' — *C. japonica* 'Billie McCaskill' X *C. oleifera* (PI 162561). Compact, upright, moderate rate of growth. Flowers are shell pink with very light pink petaloids near center. Frilly, peony form. Very hardy flower buds. Blooms late November to-mid -January. Cold hardy to –15°F.

'Winter's Charm' — *C. sasanqua* 'Takara-wase' X *C. oleifera* (PI 162561). Upright, columnar growth, with leathery, glossy dark green leaves. Flowers are lavender pink, peony form. Blooms October through November. Cold hardy to –10°F.

'Winter's Cupid' — *C. oleifera* (PI 162561) X [*C. sasanqua* 'Narumi-gata' X *C. hiemalis* 'Shishi-gashira']. Moderately upright growth. Leaves thick, leathery, semi-glossy, dark green. Heavy bud set. Flowers are white, flushed light pink near apex and on underside. Semi-double with curved and fluted petals with large central cluster of golden yellow anthers. Blooms late November through early January. Cold hardy to –15°F.

'Winter's Darling' – *C. hiemalis* 'Shishi-gashira' X *C. oleifera* 'Lu Shan Snow'. Moderately upright, slow growth. Leaves leathery semi-glossy, dark green small narrow. Flowers are deep cerise pink, two-tone miniature anemone. Blooms from November through December. Cold hardy to –10°F.

'Winter's Dream' – *C. hiemalis* 'Peach Puff' X *C. oleifera* (PI 162561). Decidedly upright, vigorous growth. Leaves leathery, dark glossy green. Flowers are pink, semi-double. Blooms from October to November. Cold hardy to –10°F.

'Winter's Fancy' – *C. hiemalis* 'Bill Wylam' X [*C. hiemalis* 'Shishi-gashira X C. oleifera (PI 162561)]. Moderately vigorous, upright and outward. This lends itself to utilization as a hedge plant. Leaves leathery, glossy dark green. Flowers are deep pink, semi-double, creped, floriferous. Blooms from October to November. Cold hardy to –5°F.

'Winter's Fire' –'Frost Prince' X *C. vernalis* 'Takarazuka'. Vigorous, upright growth with a weeping habit. Leaves semi-glossy, dark green. Flowers are medium, reddish pink, semi-double with upright star-like creased petals. Blooms from November to January. Cold hardy to –5°F.

'Winter's Hope' – *C. oleifera* 'Lu Shan Snow' X 'Frost Princess'. Moderately vigorous, upright growth. Leaves leathery, glossy, cupped, very dark green. Flowers, white, semi-double. Blooms from early October through November. Cold hardy to –10°F.

'Winter's Interlude' – *C. oleifera* (PI 162561) X *C. species* 'Pink Tea.' Moderately vigorous, upright, plant habit, leads itself to use as a hedge, since it tends to spread horizontally as well as being upright. Leaves leathery, glossy dark green. Flowers bright pink, anemone form. Blooms from November through December. Cold hardy to –15°F.'

'Winter's Joy' – [*C. sasanqua* 'Narumi-gata' X *C. hiemalis* 'Shishi-gashira] X *C. oleifera* (PI 162561). Vigorous, upright to columnar growth. Lends itself to making a tall, narrow hedge. Leaves leather, glossy, dark green. Flowers, bright pink, semi-double with crepy petal margins. Blooms from November through December. Cold hardy to –10°F.

'Winter's Moonlight' – *C. japonica* 'Tricolor Red (Seibold) X *C. oleifera* (PI 162561), Plant compact, average vigor, globular growth. Leaves dark green, glossy. Flowers are white, mostly single to anemone form. Long blooming season from early December through February. Cold hardy to –15°F.

'Winter's Peony' – *C. oleifera* (PI 162561) X [*C. sasanqua* 'Narumi-gata' X *C. hiemalis* 'Shishi-gashira']. Excellent, bushy pyramidal form without pruning or shaping. Moderate to vigorous growth. Leaves leathery, glossy, dark green. Flowers medium to light pink semi-double, to mostly peony form, floriferous. Blooms from November through December. Cold hardy to –5°F.

'Winter's Red Rider' – *C. hiemalis* 'Shishi-gashira' x *C. oleifera* 'Lu Shan Snow'. Very slow, dense, semi-dwarf, makes a good patio plant or Bonsai specimen. Leaves leathery, glossy, dark green, small. Flowers are lavender pink, single with notched petals. Blooms from Mid-October through November. Cold hardy to –10°F.

'Winter's Rose' – *C. oleifera* (PI 162561) X *C. hiemalis* 'Otome.' Plant similar to that of 'Winter's Red Rider'. Very slow, dense, semi-dwarf, with small leaves and small flowers, which makes it a good patio plant and is highly sought after for Bonsai purposes. Leaves leathery, glossy, very dark green. Flowers shell pink, formal double. Blooms from mid-October to early December. Cold hardy to –15°F.

'Winter's Snowman' — [*C. sasanqua* 'Narumi-gata'X *C. hiemalis* 'Shishi-gashira'] X *C. oleifera* (PI 162561). Vigorous, upright to columnar growth. Lends itself to making a tall, narrow hedge. Leaves leathery, semi-glossy, dark green. Flowers are white, semi-double to mostly anemone, slightly cupped. Blooms from mid-November through December. Cold hardy to –10°F.

'Winter's Star' – *C. oleifera* 'Lu Shan Snow' X *C. hiemalis* 'Showa-no-sakae'. Moderate to vigorous, upright growth. Leaves leathery, semi-glossy, medium green. Flowers are large, violet-pink, single. Blooms from very early-October through November. Cold hardy to –5°F.

'Winter's Toughie' – *C. oleifera* ' (PI 162561) X *C. sasanqua* 'Jean May'. Slow to moderate growth, somewhat spreading. Leaves thick, leathery, glossy dark green. Flower buds very hardy. Flowers are lavender pink, semi-double, fluted and notched petals. Blooms from mid November through December. Cold hardy to –15°F.

'Snow Flurry'   'Winter's Interlude'

'Snow Flurry'   'Winter's Interlude'

'Winter's Hope'

'Elaine Lee'

'Winter's Hope'

'Elaine Lee'

'Winter's Beauty'

'Winter's Beauty'

'Winter's Red Rider'   'Winter's Waterlily'

'Winter's Snowman'   'Winter's Waterlily'
                              72 hrs. after 19° F

'Winter's Waterlily' – *C. oleifera* (PI 162561) X *C. sasanqua* 'Mine-no-yuki'. Slow to moderate globular form. Leaves thick, leathery, semi-glossy, very dark green. Flowers are white anemone to formal double, and appears to be more frost resistant even when partly open than most camellias. Blooms from November through January. Cold hardy to –15°F.

Spring Blooming Hybrids

'Fire 'N Ice' – *C. japonica* 'Tricolor (Siebold) X *C. oleifera* (PI 162561). Average, dense, upright growth. Leaves very dark green, semi-glossy. Flowers are dark red-pink, medium to large semi-double to rose form double. Blooms March-April. Cold hardy to –5°F.

'Ice Follies' – *C X Williamsii* 'November Pink' X *C. oleifera* 'Lu Shan Snow'. Open, spreading, growth. Leaves dark green, semi-glossy. Flowers are bright pink, large, semi-double, crepe-like petals. Blooms March-April. Cold hardy to –5°F.

'Pink Icicle' – *C X Williamsii* 'November Pink' X *C. oleifera* 'Lu Shan Snow'. Average, compact, upright growth. Leaves dark green, glossy. Flowers are shell pink, large to very large, peony form with large rabbit ears. Blooms February to March. Cold hardy to –5°F.

'Red Fellow' – *C. japonica* 'Tricolor Red' (Siebold) X *C. oleifera* (PI 162561). Spreading, semi-compact, medium growth rate. Leaves large, dark green, glossy. Flowers are bright neon red, large, semi-double, large yellow stamen center. Blooms April to May. Cold hardy to –5°F.

'Spring Cardinal' –*C. japonica* 'Tricolor Red' (Siebold) X *C. oleifera* (PI 162561). Medium, dense, upright growth. Leaves dark green, semi-glossy. Flowers are Crimson red, formal double. Blooms February to March. Cold hardy to –10°F.

'Spring Circus' – *C. japonica* 'Tricolor Red' (Siebold) X *C. oleifera* (PI 162561). Medium, compact, upright growth. Leaves, medium green, glossy. Flowers are semi-double and vary from solid red, white or pink, to stripes and blotches of deep pink on white background, all on the same plant. Blooms April to May. Cold hardy to –10°F.

'Spring Frill' — *C. oleifera* (PI 162561) X *C. vernalis* 'Egao..' Slow, spreading growth. Leaves dull, medium green. Flowers are bright, iridescent pink, large, rose form double. Blooms April to May. Cold hardy to –10ºF.

C. Most of the U.S. National Arboretum Cultivars Developed by Dr. William Ackerman are Interspecific Hybrids Involving Two, or More, Species. However, there are Four Exceptions in the Spring Blooming *C. japonica* Series, Listed Below:

'Betty Sette' – 'Frost Queen' X 'Variety Z'. Compact, upright, average growth rate. Leaves broad, glossy, dark green. Flowers are medium pink, formal double of good substance. Late. Cold hardy to –10ºF.

'Frost Queen' – Field trial selection from seed introduced from Northern Japan. Dense, upright growth. Leaves glossy, dished, very dark green. Flowers are white, large, semi-double with good substance. Mid-season to late. Cold hardy to –5ºF.

'Jerry Hill' – 'Frost Queen X Variety Z'. Average, dense, upright growth. Leaves broad, glossy, dark green. Flowers are rose pink, formal double. Late. Cold hardy to -10ºF.

'Kuro Delight' – *C. japonica* 'Kuro Tsubaki' X 'Variety Z'. Slow, spreading growth of average density. Leaves dark blue-green, very long and narrow, peach-like in shape. Flowers are large, maroon red, semi-double to loose peony. Mid season to late. Long blooming season. Cold hardy to -15ºF.

'Spring Frill'   'Fire 'N' Ice'

'Jerry Hill'   'Red Fellow'

'Spring Cardinal'

'Betty Sette'

'Spring Circus'

(white form)

'Spring Circus'

(red form)

'Kuro Delight'   'Ice Follies'

'Kuro Delight'   'Pink Icicle'

D. In 1995, Dr. Clifford Parks Introduced the April Series of Hardy Cultivars Recommended for USDA Zone 6b:

'April Blush' – 'Berenice Boddy' X 'Dr. Tinsley'; CF-33. Compact, slow to medium growth. Flowers are shell-pink, semi-double. Blooms midseason.

'April Dawn' – 'Berenice Boddy' X 'Herme'; CF-29. Erect, vigorous growth. Flowers are shades of pink, shell, and white variegated (not virus), formal double. Blooms over long period.

'April Kiss' – 'Berenice Boddy' X 'Reg Ragland'. Compact, moderate growth rate. Flowers are small, medium red, formal double. Blooms early season.

'April Remembered' – 'Berenice Boddy' X 'Dr. Tinsley'. Vigorous, fast-growing plant. Flowers are large, cream to pink-shaded, semi-double. Blooms early to late season.

'April Rose' – 'Berenice Boddy' X 'Kumasaka'; CF-31. Compact, relatively slow growing, well-formed plant. Flowers are rose-red, formal double. Blooms medium to late season.

'April Snow' – 'Triphosa' X 'Betty Sheffield Supreme'. Compact, slow growth, well-formed plant. Flowers are white, rose-form double. Blooms late season.

'April Tryst' – Seedling of 'Yours Truly'. Erect, medium growth rate, well-formed splant. Flowers are bright red, anemone form. Hardy flower buds. Blooms midseason.

'April Blush'

'April Rose'

'April Snow'

'April Tryst'

APPENDICES

Appendix 1

CAMELLIA SOCIETIES

American Camellia Society
Ann Walton, Executive Director
100 Massee lane
Fort Valley, GA 31030, USA
Phone: 912-967-2358
FAX: 912-967-2083
Email: journal@camellias-acs.com
Home Page: www.camellias-acs.com

Affiliated with the American Horticultural Society, and the National Council of State Garden Clubs. Also, The Royal Horticultural Society and the International Camellia Society.

The American Camellia Society (ACS) can provide information about the various regional and local Camellia societies regarding their activities and periodic publications. The ACS publishes an annual Yearbook and 4 Journal publications a year (February, May, August, and November).

International Camellia Society
President: Mrs. Pat Macdonald
Westwyn, 44 Kelland Road, R.D.3 Waiuku,
NEW ZEALAND
Membership Registrar: Dr. David Razzak
Bas Sejour, Ruettes des Fries, Cobo,
Guernsey, GY5 7PW
CHANNEL ISLANDS,
Editor: Mr. Herbert Short
41 Galveston Road
East Putney, London SW15 2RZ
UNITED KINGDOM

The International Camellia Society has representatives in fourteen countries and members in twenty-six countries. The annual

Yearbook publication provides information about research and cultural activities being conducted in many parts of the world.

Appendix 2

A Short List of Retailers

American Plant Food Co., Garden Center & Nursery –
Chevy Chase Location - 5258 River Rd., Bethesda, Maryland
20816
(301)-656-3311
Beltway Location – 7405 River Rd., Bethesda, Maryland
20817
(301)-469-7690

Behnke's Nursery
Beltsville Location - 11300 Baltimore Ave. (US #1), Beltsville,
Maryland 20704
(301)-937-1100
Largo Location – 700 Watkins Pk. Dr., Largo, Maryland
20772
(301)-249-2492
Potomac Location – 9545 River Rd, Potomac, Maryland
20854
(301)-983-9200 or (301)-983-4400

Betty's Azalea Ranch
12507 Lee Highway, Fairfax, VA 22039
(703)-830-8687

Camellia Forest Nursery
125 Carolina Forest Road, Chapel Hill, NC 27516
(919)-967-5529

Chesser's Nursery
30435 Chesser Rd., Assawoman, VA 23302
(757)-824-3607

Fairweather Gardens
P. O. Box 330, Greenwich, NJ 08323
(609)-451-6261

Hill's Nursery
1722 North Glebe Road, Arlington, VA 22207
(703)-527-3472

McDonald Nurseries
1139 West Pembrook Ave., Hampton, VA 23661
(804)-722-7463 (They do not ship out of state)
Roslyn Nursery
211 Burrs Lane, Dix Hills, NY 11746
(516)-643-9347

Wholesale Only
Bennett Creek Nursery, Inc.
3613 Bridge Road, Suffolk, VA 23435
(757)-483-1425, (800)-343-4611, FAX: (757)-483-9058
Big Frog Nursery
Columbus Location - P.O. Box 691, 1350 Leecudd Rd.,
Columbus, NC 28722,
Rutherford Location -Rutherfordton, NC 28139,
(888)-252-3764
Fax: (828)-863-2966, Email: bigfrog@alltel.net
Bond Nursery, Corp.
6420 Del Norte Lane, Dallas, TX 75225
(214)-739-8586
Briggs Nursery, Inc.
4407 Henderson Blvd., Olympia, WA 98501
1-800-999-9972
Cam Too Camellia Nursery
805 Oakbury Court, Greensboro, NC 27455
1-800-758-8121 or (910)-643-3727, FAX: (336)-643-0840
Flowerwood Nursery ,
Brookville Location - 17300 Powell Rd, Brookville, FL 34601,
(800)-783-3559 or FAX: (352)-754-2425
Bushnell Location - 2792 County Rd, #564, Bushnell, FL
33513,
(800)-426-0732 or FAX: (352)-783-1726
Glenn Read Nursery
1141 West Fire Dept. Road, Lucedale, Mississippi 39452
(601)-947-6592, FAX: (601)-947-1835
EMAIL: grcamsan@ametro.net

Hines Nursery, Inc.
Vacaville Location - 3920 Lagoon Valley Rd., Vacaville, CA, 95688
(800)-777-1097 or FAX: (707)-446-9435
Winters Location - 8633 Winters Rd, Winters, CA 95694, (800)-737-8140 or FAX: (530)-795-6035
Monrovia Nursery, Inc.
Azusa Location - P.O. Box Q, Azusa, CA 91702-1336
(800)-999-9321 or FAX: (626)-334-3126
Oregon Location - (800)-666-9321 or FAX: (503)-868-7352
Plant Development Services, 17325 County Rd., #68, Loxley, AL 36551
(888)-922-7374, EMAIL: rfrench@plantdevelopment.com
Tarheel Native Trees
4339 Peele Rd., Clayton, NC 27520. (919)-553-5927
FAX: (919)-553-0146
Tom Dodd Nurseries
P.O. Drawer 45, U.S. Highway 98, Semmes, Al 3657
(888)-866-3633, or FAX: (334)-649-1965

Appendix 3

Collections and Gardens North of the Camellia Belt

American Horticultural Society, River Farm
(Associated with the 500-acre estate of George Washington)
7931 East Boulevard Drive, Alexandria, VA 22308-1300
(703)-768-5700

Bartram's Garden, John Bartram Association
54th Street and Lindbergh Boulevard, Philadelphia, PA 19143
(215)-7299-5281

Bernard's Inn Farm, Polly Hill Association
Martha's Vineyard, North Tisbury, MA 02568

Bon Air Park
850 N. Lexington St., Arlington, VA
Department of Community Affairs, (703)-558-2152

Brooklyn Botanic Garden
1000 Washington Avenue, Brooklyn, NY 11225

Brookside Gardens
1800 Glenallen Avenue, Wheaton, Maryland 20902
(301)-949-8230

Greenspring Gardens and Park
4601 Greenspring Road, Alexandria, VA 22312

Hillwood Grounds and Museum
4155 Linnean Avenue, NW, Washington, DC
(202)-686-5807

Londontown Publik House and Gardens
839 Londontown Road, Edgewater, Maryland 21037
(301)-222-1919

Longwood Gardens
P.O. Box 501, 409 Conservatory Rd,
Kennett Square, PA 19348

McCrillis Gardens & Gallery
6910 Greentree Road, Bethesda, Maryland 20817
(301)-365-5728

Missouri Botanical Garden, St. Louis, MO 63101
The first garden of its kind established in the United States.
Founded in 1859

Planting Fields Arboretum
P.O. Box 58, Oyster Bay, NY 11771
U.S. National Arboretum
3500 New York Avenue, Washington, DC 20002
(202)-245-4523

Appendix 4

REFERENCES AND SUGGESTED READINGS

Ackerman, W. L.
1971 GENETIC AND CYTOLOGICAL STUDIES WITH CAMELLIA AND RELATED GENERA. U.S. Agricultural Research Service Technical Bulletin #1427. 115 pp.

1973 SPECIES COMPATIBILITY RELATIONSHIPS IN THE GENUS CAMELLIA. *Jour. of Heredity* 64: 356-358.

1977 WINTER INJURY IN THE NATIONAL ARBORETUM CAMELLIA COLLECTION DURING THE 1976-77 SEASON. *Amer. CamelliaYearbook* 1977: 14-21.

1978 NATIONAL ARBORETUM CAMELLIAS AND THE 1977-78 WINTER SEASON. *Amer. Camellia Yearbook* 1978: 25-26.

1978 THE CAMELLIA SASANQUA DILEMMA—ARE C.OLEIFERA HYBRIDS THE ANSWER? *Amer. Camellia Yearbook* 1978: 117-121.

1981 EXTENDING THE RANGE OF FALL FLOWERING CAMELLIAS NORTHWARD. *Amer. Camellia Journal* 36(4): 5,6.

1987 CHANGING OLD HABITS -TO BREAK OR NOT TO BREAK THE TAP ROOT. *Amer. Camellia Journal* 42(1): 20.

1989 HISTORY AND PROGRESS ON COLD HARDINESS WITH CAMELLIAS IN NORTHEASTERN UNITED STATES. *International Camellia Society Journal* 21:81-84.

1993 CAMELLIAS FOR COLDER CLIMATES. *Horticulture* LXXI(5):28-30

1994 THE 1993-94 SEASON: THE UTLIMATE IN TEST WINTERS. *Amer. Camellia Yearbook* 42-44.

1995 SOME PROBLEMS EVALUATING CAMELLIAS FOR COLD HARDINESS. *Amer. Camellia Journal* 50(4): 16-18.

1995 CAMELLIA CULTIVARS THAT HAVE WITHSTOOD THE TEST OF TIME IN THE WASHINGTON, DC AREA. *Amer. Camellia Journal.* 50(4): 22.

1997 THE EXPERIMENTAL CAMELLIA GARDEN OF BON AIR PARK, ARLINGTON, VA. *Amer. Camellia Journal* 52(3): 26-27

1998 NOT ALL CAMELLIA OLEIFERAS ARE EQUAL. *Amer. Camellia Journal* 53(1): 8-9

1998 COLD HARDY SPRING BLOOMING CAMELLIAS. *Amer. Camellia Yearbook* 1998: 46-48

2000 NORTHERN EXPOSURE. *Amer. Nurseryman*, Dec. 1st. Vol. 192(11):388-43.

Ackerman, W.L. and K. Conrad.

1995 CAMELLIA OLEIFERA 'LU SHAN SNOW' - AN OUTSTANDING SPECIMEN. *Amer. Camellia Journal* 50(2): 2-3.

_____ and M. Williams.

1980 EXTENDING THE CLIMATIC RANGE OF CAMELLIAS. International Camellia Journal 12: 10-11.

1982 INTERGENERIC CROSSES WITHIN THEACEAE AND THE SUCCESSFUL HYBRIDIZATION OF CAMELLIA JAPONICA AND CAMELLIA SASANQUA WITH FRANKLINIA ALATAMAHA.*HortScience* 17(4): 566-569.

_____ and A.L. Zhang.

1983 DISTINGUISHING CAMELLIA SPECIES USING DORSAL LEAF SURFACE IMPRESSIONS. *Jour. Amer. Soc. Hort. Sci.* 108(3): 439-444.

Barczak, P.J.

1978 CAMELLIAS AT PLANTING FIELDS ARBORETUM. *Amer. CamelliaYearbook.* 1978: 82-86

Barden, W. H., Jr.

1974 CAMELLIAS IN THE NORTHEAST. *Amer. Camellia Yearbook* 1974 II: 53-56.

Baxter, L.W., Jr.

1991 THE FATE OF CAMELLIAS CUT BACK IN THE AUTUMN. *Amer. Camellia Journal.* 47(1): 12-13.

Bernstein, M. D.

1978 GROWING CAMELLIAS OUTDOORS IN NEW YORK CITY. *Amer.Camellia Yearbook* 1978: 178-184.

1982 AN UPDATE ON GROWING CAMELLIAS OUTDOORS IN NEW YORK CITY. *Amer. Camellia Yearbook* 1982: 86-92.

Callaway, D.J. and M.B., Editors

   2000 BREEDING ORNAMENTAL PLANTS, CH.14 'BREEDING
   CAMELLIAS.' Timber Press, Portland, OR.

Carter, E.P.

   1956 COLD RESISTANCE AND CARE OF OUTDOOR
   CAMELLIAS IN NORTHERN LATITUDES. *Amer. Camellia
   Yearbook* 1956: 82-91.

Chang, H.T. and B. Bartholomew.

   1984 CAMELLIAS (A NEW REVISION OF THE GENUS
   CAMELLIA). Timber Press, Portland, OR. 211 pp.

Creech, J.L. and F. DeVos.

   1958 EXTENDING THE CULTURAL RANGE OF CAMELLIAS.
   Amer. Camellia Yearbook 1958: 34-38.

Edgar, L.A

   1991 CAMELLIAS: A COMPLETE GUIDE. The Crowood Press.
   224 pp.

Feathers, D. L. and M. H. Brown, Editors.

   1978 THE CAMELLIA, ITS HISTORY, CULTURE, GENETICS,
   AND A LOOK INTO ITS FUTURE DEVELOPMENT. R.L.
   Bryan Co. Columbia, SC. 476 pp.

Garner, R.L.

   1988 THE GRAFTER'S HANDBOOK. Cassell Publishers, Ltd.
   London. 323 pp.

Gonos, A. and S. Bracci, Editors

   1999 CAMELLIA NOMENCLATURE. Southern California
   Camellia Society, Inc. Arcadia, CA. 184 pp.

Hill, M.L.

   1970 ADAPTATION OF CAMELLIAS SPECIES TO MARTHA'S
   VINEYARD. *Amer. Camellia Yearbook.* 1970: 46-55.

   1979 THE CAMELLIA COLLECTION AT BARNARD'S INN
   FARM AND HOW IT CAME TO BE. *Amer. Camellia
   Yearbook* 1979:172-177.

Howard, J.F., Dr.

   1965 MICRO-CLIMATES AND HOW THEY AFFECT PLANT
   HARDINESS. *Amer. Camellia Yearbook.* 1965: 151-159

Jiyin, G.

    1999 THE PRESENT STATUS OF CAMELLIA DEVELOPMENT IN CHINA. *Amer. Camellia Journal.* 54(2): 18-19.

Levi, W.M.

    1955 VARIETAL DIFFERENCES IN COLD RESISTANCE OF FLOWER BUDS. *Amer. Camellia Yearbook.* 1955: 255-271. Followup articles in *Amer. Camellia Yearbooks*: 1958, 1960, 1962, 1964, 1967, 1969, 1970, 1971, 1972, & 1973.

Ling, C.T.

    1977 WHAT HAPPENED TO CAMELLIAS OUTDOORS IN Maryland LAST WINTER? *Amer. Camellia Yearbook.* 1977: 21-23.

    1978 WINTER IN BALTIMORE. *Amer. Camellia Yearbook.* 1978: 23-24.

Maryott, A.A.

    1969 COLD HARDINESS OF CAMELLIAS IN THE WASHINGTON-BALTIMORRE AREA. *Amer. Camellia Yearbook.* 1969: 75-78.

Meyer, F.G.

    1959. PLANT EXPLORATIONS. Crops Research ARS 34-9. USDA.

Parks, C.R.

    1968 PROGRESS TOWARDS THE DEVELOPMENT OF A MORE COLD RESISTANT CAMELLIA. *Amer. Camellia Yearbook.* 1968:206-215.

    1972 DEVELOPING A BASIS FOR SELECTING MORE WINTER TOLERANT CAMELLIAS. Amer. Camellia Yearbook. 1972: 388-42.

    1978 THE COMPONENTS OF COLD HARDINESS IN CAMELLIAS. *Amer. Camellia Yearbook.* 1978: 47-55.

    1984 THE WINTER HARDINESS OF INTERSPECIFIC CAMELLIA HYBRIDS. *Amer. Camellia Yearbook.* 1984: 54-59.

    1990 CROSS COMPATABILITY STUDIES IN THE GENUS CAMELLIA. *International Camellia Soc. Jrnl.* 22:; 37-54.

_____ and J.D. Doyle.
1983 PATTERNS OF WINTER INJURY IN CAMELLIA JAPONICA. *Amer. Camellia Yearbook*. 1983: 39-44.
_____ and K. M. Parks.
1993 BREEDING CAMELLIAS FOR GARDEN CUTURE. *Amer. Camellia Yearbook*. 1993: 1-8.
Presnall, C.C. and M. H. Brown.
1959 WINTER HARDINESS OF CAMELLIAS IN THE WASHINGTON, DC METROPOLITAN AREA. *Amer. Camellia Yearbook*. 1959: 225-235.
Presnall, C.C.
1964 COLD HARDY CAMELLIAS IN OUR NATION'S CAPITAL. *Amer. Camellia Yearbook*. 1964:75-79
Rolfe, J.
1992 GARDENING WITH CAMELLIAS-A NEW ZEALAND GUIDE. Godwit Press, Ltd. Auckland, New Zealand. 176 pp.
Savige, T.J.
1993 THE INTERNATIONAL CAMELLIA REGISTER. Kyodo Printing Co., Pte, Ltd., Singapore. 2209 pp.
Sealey, Robert J.
1958 A REVISION OF THE GENUS CAMELLIA. The Royal Horticultural Society, London. 239 pp.
Sewell, M.M. and C. R. Parks.
1981 A NEW PROGRAM TO MEASURE HARDINESS IN CAMELLIA. *Amer. Camellia Yearbook*. 1981: 121-134.
Trehane, J.
1998 CAMELLIAS. Timber Press. Portland, OR. 176 pp.
Try, R.A.
1965 THE CAMELLIA AS A HARDY SHRUB. *Amer. Camellia Yearbook*.1965: 87-93.
Warner, D.C.
1973 GROWING CAMELLIAS OUT OF DOORS IN SOUTHERN CONNECTICUT. *Amer. Camellia Yearbook*. 1973: 41-44.
Weiser, C.J.
1970 COLD RESISTANCE AND INJURY IN WOODY PLANTS. *Science* 169: 1269.

Worman, J.G.

    1959 CAMELLIA PROPAGATION AT GLENN DALE PLANT INTRODUCTION STATION. *Amer.Camellia Yearbook.* 1959:103-114

Xia, L., A.L. Zhang and T.J. Xiao

    1993 AN INTRODUCTION TO THE UTILIZATION OF CAMELLIA OIL IN CHINA. *Amer. Camellia Yearbook.* 1993: 112-115.

Zimmerman, P.W.

    1948 HARDINESS IN CAMELLIAS. *Amer. Camellia Yearbook.* 1948: 106-107,109.

    1949 MORE ABOUT HARDY CAMELLIAS. Amer. Camellia Yearbook.1949: 212-213.

    1953 HARDY CAMELLIAS IN THE VICINITY OF NEW YORK CITY. *Amer. Camellia Yearbook.* 1953: 313-319.

    1955 CAMELLIAS IN NEW YORK. *Amer. Camellia Yearbook.* 1955: 225-231

Book Chapters Written by William L. Ackerman

1965 "The Introduction of New Plants from Foreign Lands," in the *Garden Journal*, New York Botanic Garden.

1972 "Breeding Plants for Beauty, Form, and Survival." U.S. Dept. Agriculture Yearbook.

1974 "Breeding New Hybrid Races of Camellia" in *Breeding Plants for Home and Garden*, Brooklyn Botanic Garden.

1977 "Breeding New Types of Camellia" (in Japanese with English Titles), *Tsubaki*, the Japan Camellia Society.

1978 "Hybridization and Genetics" and "Research and Experimentation" in the *Camellia*. Editors, Feathers and Brown, The RL. Bryan Co., Columbia, SC.

1981 "Recent Breeding Developments in Camellias in the United States" (in Japanese), *Garden Life of Japan*.

1995 "Cold Hardy Camellias" in *Shade Gardening*. Time Life Books.

2000 "Breeding Camellias." *Breeding Ornamental Plants*, ed. Dorothy and Brett Calloway. Timber Press, Portland, Oregon.

2002 Revision and update of the 1978 publication *Camellias* by Feathers and Brown. "Hybridization and Genetics" and "Cold Hardiness" (completely new chapter). To be published by Timber Press.

INDICES

Cultivars by Species

C. hiemalis
Kanjiro 15, 91
Showa-no-sakae 91, 100

C. japonica
April Blush 16, 110
April Dawn 16, 110
April Kiss 110
April Remembered 16, 110
April Rose 16, 110
April Snow 16, 110
April Tryst 16, 110
Berenice Boddy 13, 14, 87, 110
Betty Sette 106
Blood of China 13, 14, 87
Bob Hope 15
C.M. Hovey 87
C.M. Wilson 13, 87
Compte de Gomer 11
Daikagura 87
Donckelarii 13, 14, 88
Dr. Tinsley 13, 14, 88, 110
Eleanor Hagood 88
Elegans (Chandler) 11, 13, 14, 87, 88
Flame 14, 88
Frost Queen 14, 95, 106
Glen 40 14, 88
Governor Mouton 13, 14, 88
Herme 14, 15, 88, 110
Jarvis Red 14
Jerry Hill 106
Kumasaka 11, 13, 14, 88, 110
Kuro Delight 106
Lady Clare 13, 14, 88
Lady Vansittart 13, 14, 88
Leucantha 13, 14, 88
Madame Lebois 11
Magnoliaeflora 88
Mathotiana 14, 88
Meredith 90
Monjisu 90
Mrs. Bertha Harmes 47, 95
Paulette Goddard 13, 14, 90
Pink Perfection 14, 90

Professor Charles Sargent 90
Purity 14
R.L. Wheeler 13, 90
Rev. John C. Drayton 13
Tricolor (Siebold) 14, 88, 90, 105
Tricolor (Siebold) Red 13, 14, 105
Variety Z 11, 13, 106
Ville de Nantes 14
White Empress 14, 90
White Queen 14

C. oleifera and its Hybrids
Fall Blooming
  Ashton's Ballet 95
  Ashton's Pink 95
  Ashton's Pride 95
  Ashton's Snow 95
  Elaine Lee 95
  Fairweather Favorite 94, 95
  Frost Prince 17, 95, 99
  Frost Princess 17, 84, 98, 99
  Lu Shan Snow 18, 47, 93, 94
  Polar Ice 98
  Snow Flurry 98
  Winter's Beauty 94, 98
  Winter's Charm 98
  Winter's Cupid 98
  Winter's Darling 98
  Winter's Dream 99
  Winter's Fancy 99
  Winter's Fire 99
  Winter's Hope 99
  Winter's Interlude 30, 99
  Winter's Joy 99
  Winter's Moonlight 94, 99
  Winter's Peony 100
  Winter's Red Rider 100
  Winter's Rose 29, 30, 100
  Winter's Snowman 100
  Winter's Star 100
  Winter's Toughie 100
  Winter's Waterlily 105

General Index

L

Levi, W.M. 10
Ling, C.T. 13
Lipton Tea Company 7
Longwood Gardens 16
Los Angeles State
  and County Arboretum 15

M

Maryott, A. 13
Meyer, Frederick 5
Mice 54
Microfoam 14, 27, 37, 39, 40, 41
Miller,W. 13
Morgan, Delbert x

N

New Jersey 6, 11, 45
North Carolina 11
Northern Vietnam 4
Nuccio's Nurseries 77

P

Parks, Clifford 10, 15, 110
Peoples Republic
    of China 4, 17, 78, 93, 94
Pioneer Camellia Society 13, 14, 31
Plant Quarantine 16, 17
Portuguese 5
Propagation 20, 63
  asexual 63
Pumphrey, John 13

R

Rabbits 53, 54
Rhododendrons xi
Rodents 26, 53, 54
Rooting Cuttings 63
Rootone 64

S

Savannah, Georgia 5

Sealy, J. Robert 2
Seed germination 49, 73
Shinto Shrines 2
Shrews 54
South Carolina 7
  Charleston 5
  University of 7
Southern California Camellia Society 7

T

Tea ceremony 1
Trading companies
  Dutch 5
  English 5
  Portuguese 5

U

U.S. National Arboretum
    5, 11, 13, 16, 17, 29, 30, 93, 106, 122
U.S. Plant Introduction Station 16
University of Washington 11

V

Voles 54

W

Waltz, Emerson 13
Washington Camellia Society 14
Westchester, New York 11

Y

Yunnan province 4

Z

Zimmerman, P.W. 11, 128

ATLANTIC PROVINCES HARDINESS ZONE MAP

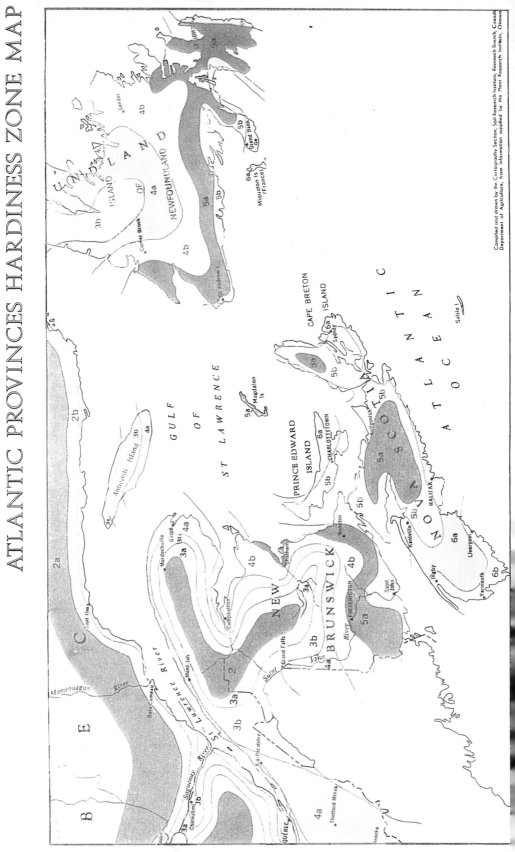

Compiled and drawn by the Cartography Section, Soil Research Institute, Research Branch, Canada Department of Agriculture, from information supplied by the Plant Research Institute, Ottawa